Created by <u>Xspurts.com</u>

Get A Free Book At: <u>xspurts.com/posts/free-book-offer</u>

Table of Contents:

Table of Contents:

Building Healthy Work Culture

Understanding the importance of a healthy work culture

Instilling the right values

Effecting a positive shift in attitudes

The Role of Leadership in a Healthy Work Environment

Inspiring trust and respect

Promoting transparency and open communication

Encouraging teamwork and collaboration

Pacing Work Responsibly

Recognizing signs of overworking

Implementing sensible working hours

Ensuring regular breaks

Respect and Equality in the Workplace

Instilling a respect culture

Promoting equality and diversity

Preventing discrimination and harassment

Work-Life Balance

Importance of work-life balance for employees

Encouraging timely offs and vacations

Setting realistic expectations

Employee Wellness Programs

Benefits of wellness programs

Suggestions for effective programs

Inviting employee participation

Office Space Design and Its Impact

How architecture affects mood and productivity

Enhancing office aesthetics

Achieving a comfortable workspace

Encouraging Skill Development

Fostering talent and potential

Importance of continued learning

Implementing practical training

Feedback and Recognition

Creating a culture of regular feedback

Recognizing employee accomplishments

How to give positive and constructive feedback

Handling Conflict

Pre-emptively addressing potential conflicts

Fairly resolving disputes

Promoting reconciliation and cooperation

Workplace Policies and Rules

Instituting sensible and clear rules

Enforcing policies justly

Regularly reviewing and updating policies

Effective Communication

Facilitating open dialogue

Addressing communication barriers

Improving listening skills

Mental Health Support At Work

Encouraging mental health awareness

Providing support systems

Promoting employee resilience

Building Trust in a Healthy Work Environment

Avoiding micromanagement

Encouraging mutual respect

Ensuring transparency

Sustainability in the Workplace

Going green for better productivity

Encouraging employee involvement

Have Questions / Comments?
Get Another Book Free

Building Healthy Work Culture

Building a healthy work culture is essential for organizations to thrive and for employees to flourish. It encompasses various elements such as fostering open communication, promoting work-life balance, prioritizing employee well-being, and fostering a sense of belongingness and inclusion. By prioritizing these aspects, organizations can create a positive and supportive work environment where employees feel valued, motivated, and engaged.

One crucial aspect of building a healthy work culture is fostering open communication. Encouraging transparent communication channels where employees feel comfortable expressing their ideas, concerns, and feedback fosters trust and collaboration within the organization. This can be achieved through regular team meetings, one-on-one check-ins, and anonymous suggestion boxes, among other methods. When employees feel heard and valued, they are more likely to feel engaged and invested in their work.

Another key component of a healthy work culture is promoting work-life balance. Recognizing the importance of personal well-being and providing resources and support to help employees manage their workloads and personal responsibilities is essential. This may include offering flexible work arrangements, providing access to mental health resources, and encouraging employees to take breaks and vacations. By prioritizing work-life balance, organizations can prevent burnout and promote overall employee satisfaction and retention.

Prioritizing employee well-being is also crucial for building a healthy work culture. This involves providing resources and support to help employees maintain their physical, mental, and emotional health. This can include offering wellness programs, access to counseling services, and promoting healthy lifestyle habits. When employees feel supported in their well-being, they are more likely to perform at their best and contribute positively to the organization.

Fostering a sense of belongingness and inclusion is another important aspect of building a healthy work culture. This involves creating an environment where all employees feel valued, respected, and included, regardless of their background or identity. This can be achieved by implementing diversity and inclusion initiatives, promoting awareness and education around issues of diversity and equity, and providing opportunities for employees to participate in affinity groups and employee resource networks. When employees feel a sense of belongingness and inclusion, they are more likely to be engaged and committed to their work and the organization.

Furthermore, promoting a culture of recognition and appreciation is essential for building a healthy work culture. Recognizing and celebrating employees' contributions and achievements fosters a positive and supportive work environment where employees feel valued and motivated. This can be done through formal recognition programs, such as employee of the month awards, as well as informal gestures of appreciation, such as thank-you notes and public recognition in team meetings. By acknowledging and rewarding employees' efforts, organizations can reinforce positive behaviors and cultivate a culture of appreciation and gratitude.

In conclusion, building a healthy work culture is essential for organizations to attract and retain top talent, foster employee engagement and productivity, and ultimately achieve success. By prioritizing open communication, promoting work-life balance, prioritizing employee well-being, fostering a sense of belongingness and inclusion, and promoting a culture of recognition and appreciation, organizations can create a positive and supportive work environment where employees can thrive and succeed.

Understanding the importance of a healthy work culture

A healthy work culture is vital for the success and well-being of both employees and organizations. It encompasses various factors that contribute to a positive and supportive work environment, including open communication, work-life balance, employee well-being, belongingness and inclusion, and recognition and appreciation. Understanding the importance of a healthy work culture is essential for achieving organizational goals, fostering employee satisfaction and engagement, and promoting overall success.

One key reason why a healthy work culture is important is its impact on employee satisfaction and engagement. When employees feel valued, supported, and respected in their work environment, they are more likely to be satisfied with their jobs and committed to the organization's goals. This leads to higher levels of employee engagement, productivity, and performance, ultimately contributing to the organization's success.

Moreover, a healthy work culture is essential for attracting and retaining top talent. In today's competitive job market, organizations that prioritize employee well-being and provide a positive work environment have a competitive advantage in attracting and retaining skilled and talented employees. Candidates are more likely to choose employers that offer a supportive work culture where they can thrive and grow professionally.

Furthermore, a healthy work culture contributes to employee well-being and overall mental and emotional health. By promoting work-life balance, providing resources and support for employee well-being, and fostering a sense of belongingness and inclusion, organizations can help employees maintain a healthy work-life balance and prevent burnout and stress. This leads to improved employee morale, reduced absenteeism, and better overall health outcomes.

Additionally, a healthy work culture enhances collaboration, teamwork, and communication within the organization. When employees feel comfortable expressing their ideas, concerns, and feedback, and when they feel included and valued as part of a team, they are more likely to collaborate effectively and communicate openly. This leads to improved decision-making, problem-solving, and innovation, driving the organization's success.

Moreover, a healthy work culture promotes organizational resilience and adaptability. In today's fast-paced and ever-changing business environment, organizations need to be agile and adaptable to stay competitive. A positive work culture that values flexibility, creativity, and continuous learning enables organizations to adapt to changing circumstances and thrive in dynamic markets.

Furthermore, a healthy work culture fosters a positive reputation and brand image for the organization. Employees who are satisfied and engaged in their work are more likely to speak positively about their employer and recommend it to others as a great place to work. This enhances the organization's reputation as an employer of choice, attracting top talent and strengthening its brand in the marketplace.

In conclusion, understanding the importance of a healthy work culture is essential for achieving organizational success, fostering employee satisfaction and engagement, and promoting overall well-being. By prioritizing open communication, work-life balance, employee well-being, belongingness and inclusion, and recognition and appreciation, organizations can create a positive and supportive work environment where employees can thrive and succeed.

Instilling the right values

Instilling the right values within an organization is crucial for achieving a healthy work environment and fostering a positive organizational culture. Values serve as guiding principles that shape attitudes, behaviors, and decision-making processes within the workplace. By instilling the right values, organizations can promote ethical conduct, teamwork, accountability, and mutual respect, which are essential for creating a supportive and productive work environment.

One of the key values that organizations should instill is integrity. Integrity involves honesty, transparency, and ethical behavior in all aspects of work. When employees uphold integrity as a core value, they act with honesty and transparency in their interactions with colleagues, clients, and stakeholders. This fosters trust and credibility within the organization, leading to stronger relationships and a more positive work environment.

Another important value to instill is teamwork. Emphasizing the importance of collaboration, cooperation, and collective effort encourages employees to work together towards common goals. When employees value teamwork, they are more willing to share knowledge, support each other, and contribute to the success of the team. This promotes a sense of camaraderie and unity within the organization, leading to increased productivity and innovation.

Accountability is another crucial value that organizations should prioritize. Holding oneself and others accountable for their actions and responsibilities fosters a culture of accountability and ownership within the workplace. When employees take ownership of their work and hold themselves accountable for their performance, they strive for excellence and take pride in their contributions. This leads to improved performance and outcomes for the organization as a whole.

Respect is also a fundamental value that organizations should instill. Respecting the diversity, opinions, and contributions of others creates a culture of inclusivity and mutual respect within the workplace. When employees feel valued and respected, they are more likely to collaborate effectively, communicate openly, and contribute their unique perspectives and ideas. This promotes creativity, innovation, and overall success within the organization.

Additionally, organizations should instill a value of continuous learning and growth. Emphasizing the importance of learning, development, and personal growth encourages employees to seek out opportunities for skill enhancement and professional advancement. When employees are committed to continuous learning, they adapt to change more effectively, stay relevant in their roles, and contribute to the organization's long-term success.

Moreover, organizations should prioritize a value of customer focus. Putting the needs and satisfaction of customers at the forefront of decision-making processes ensures that products and services meet customer expectations and deliver value. When employees are customer-focused, they strive to exceed customer expectations, build strong relationships, and drive customer loyalty. This ultimately contributes to the organization's reputation, competitiveness, and profitability.

In conclusion, instilling the right values within an organization is essential for achieving a healthy work environment and fostering a positive organizational culture. Values such as integrity, teamwork, accountability, respect, continuous learning, and customer focus serve as guiding principles that shape attitudes, behaviors, and decision-making processes within the workplace. By prioritizing these values, organizations can create a supportive and productive work environment where employees thrive and contribute to the organization's success.

Effecting a positive shift in attitudes

Effecting a positive shift in attitudes is essential for achieving a healthy work environment and fostering a positive organizational culture. Attitudes play a significant role in shaping employees' perceptions, behaviors, and interactions within the workplace. By promoting positive attitudes such as optimism, resilience, open-mindedness, and collaboration, organizations can create a supportive and empowering work environment where employees feel motivated, engaged, and valued.

One way to effect a positive shift in attitudes is by promoting optimism and positivity within the workplace. Encouraging employees to maintain a positive outlook, focus on solutions rather than problems, and approach challenges with optimism can create a more upbeat and resilient work environment. Optimistic attitudes not only improve morale and motivation but also contribute to higher levels of creativity, innovation, and problem-solving.

Furthermore, promoting resilience and adaptability among employees is crucial for fostering a positive work environment. Resilience involves the ability to bounce back from setbacks, cope with adversity, and thrive in the face of change. By providing resources and support to help employees develop resilience skills, organizations can create a culture that encourages growth, learning, and continuous improvement. Resilient employees are better equipped to handle stress, overcome obstacles, and maintain high levels of performance and well-being.

Moreover, fostering open-mindedness and a willingness to embrace change is essential for effecting a positive shift in attitudes. In today's fast-paced and ever-changing business environment, organizations need employees who are open to new ideas, perspectives, and ways of working. Encouraging open-mindedness promotes a culture of innovation, collaboration, and continuous learning, where employees feel empowered to challenge the status quo, explore new opportunities, and adapt to changing circumstances.

Additionally, promoting collaboration and teamwork among employees is key to creating a positive work environment. Encouraging employees to work together, share ideas, and support each other fosters a sense of camaraderie and unity within the organization. Collaboration promotes creativity, innovation, and problem-solving, as diverse perspectives and skills are brought together to tackle challenges and achieve common goals.

Furthermore, promoting empathy and understanding among employees is essential for fostering a positive work environment. Empathy involves recognizing and understanding the feelings and perspectives of others, which helps build strong relationships and foster mutual respect and trust. Encouraging employees to practice empathy promotes a culture of inclusivity, respect, and support, where individuals feel valued and understood.

Moreover, promoting a culture of gratitude and appreciation can also contribute to a positive shift in attitudes within the workplace. Recognizing and acknowledging employees' contributions, accomplishments, and efforts fosters a sense of appreciation and motivation. Gratitude promotes a culture of positivity, kindness, and generosity, where employees feel valued and inspired to go above and beyond in their work.

In conclusion, effecting a positive shift in attitudes is essential for achieving a healthy work environment and fostering a positive organizational culture. By promoting attitudes such as optimism, resilience, open-mindedness, collaboration, empathy, and gratitude, organizations can create a supportive and empowering work environment where employees feel motivated, engaged, and valued. Cultivating these attitudes not only enhances employee well-being and satisfaction but also contributes to organizational success and growth.

The Role of Leadership in a Healthy Work Environment

Leadership plays a crucial role in creating and maintaining a healthy work environment within an organization. Effective leaders set the tone for the workplace culture, inspire employees, and drive organizational success. They play a key role in fostering open communication, promoting collaboration, prioritizing employee well-being, and instilling a sense of purpose and belonging among team members.

One of the primary responsibilities of leadership in creating a healthy work environment is to establish clear communication channels. Effective leaders communicate openly and transparently with employees, sharing information about organizational goals, strategies, and expectations. By fostering open communication, leaders encourage employees to share their ideas, concerns, and feedback, creating a culture of trust and transparency within the organization.

Moreover, leadership plays a critical role in promoting collaboration and teamwork within the workplace. Effective leaders encourage collaboration by fostering a culture of mutual respect, trust, and cooperation among team members. They provide opportunities for employees to work together towards common goals, recognize and celebrate team achievements, and promote a sense of camaraderie and unity within the organization.

Furthermore, leadership plays a vital role in prioritizing employee well-being and creating a supportive work environment. Effective leaders prioritize the physical, mental, and emotional well-being of employees by providing resources and support for work-life balance, mental health, and personal development. They lead by example, modeling healthy behaviors and promoting a culture of self-care and wellness within the organization.

Additionally, leadership plays a crucial role in instilling a sense of purpose and belonging among employees. Effective leaders inspire and motivate employees by articulating a compelling vision for the organization and aligning individual goals with organizational objectives. They create opportunities for employees to contribute meaningfully to the organization's success and recognize and celebrate their contributions, fostering a sense of pride and belonging among team members.

Furthermore, leadership plays a vital role in promoting diversity, equity, and inclusion within the workplace. Effective leaders recognize the value of diversity and actively work to create an inclusive work environment where all employees feel valued, respected, and supported. They champion diversity initiatives, promote awareness and education around issues of diversity and equity, and hold themselves and others accountable for creating a culture of inclusivity within the organization.

Moreover, leadership plays a critical role in promoting a culture of accountability and continuous improvement within the organization. Effective leaders hold themselves and others accountable for their actions, decisions, and performance, setting clear expectations and providing feedback and support to help employees succeed. They foster a culture of learning and growth by encouraging employees to take ownership of their development, seek out opportunities for skill enhancement, and learn from mistakes and setbacks.

In conclusion, leadership plays a crucial role in creating and maintaining a healthy work environment within an organization. Effective leaders set the tone for the workplace culture, inspire employees, and drive organizational success by fostering open communication, promoting collaboration, prioritizing employee well-being, instilling a sense of purpose and belonging, championing diversity and inclusion, and promoting accountability and continuous improvement. By demonstrating these qualities and behaviors, leaders can create a positive and supportive work environment where employees thrive and contribute to the organization's success.

Inspiring trust and respect

Inspiring trust and respect is essential for achieving a healthy work environment and fostering positive relationships among team members. Trust and respect are foundational elements that contribute to open communication, collaboration, and mutual support within the workplace. Effective leaders play a key role in inspiring trust and respect by demonstrating integrity, empathy, transparency, and fairness in their actions and interactions with others.

One of the primary ways leaders inspire trust and respect is by demonstrating integrity in their words and actions. Integrity involves honesty, reliability, and ethical behavior in all aspects of work. When leaders consistently uphold their commitments, act with transparency, and demonstrate ethical conduct, they earn the trust and respect of their team members. Employees feel confident in their leaders' integrity and are more likely to follow their guidance and direction.

Moreover, leaders inspire trust and respect by demonstrating empathy and understanding towards their team members. Empathy involves recognizing and understanding the feelings and perspectives of others, which helps build strong relationships and foster mutual respect and trust. When leaders show empathy towards their employees, they create a supportive work environment where individuals feel valued, heard, and understood. This promotes a sense of belonging and loyalty among team members.

Transparency is another key factor in inspiring trust and respect within the workplace. Leaders who are transparent and open about organizational goals, decisions, and challenges build credibility and trust among their team members. Transparency fosters a culture of honesty and accountability, where employees feel informed and empowered to contribute their ideas and feedback. This leads to greater engagement, collaboration, and innovation within the organization.

Furthermore, leaders inspire trust and respect by treating all employees fairly and equitably. Fairness involves making decisions based on merit, without bias or favoritism, and treating all employees with dignity and respect. When leaders demonstrate fairness in their actions, they create a level playing field where everyone has an equal opportunity to succeed. Employees feel valued and respected when they are treated fairly, which strengthens their trust and loyalty towards their leaders.

In addition, leaders inspire trust and respect by fostering a culture of recognition and appreciation within the workplace. Recognizing and acknowledging employees' contributions, accomplishments, and efforts builds morale and motivation and reinforces positive behaviors. When leaders show appreciation for their team members' hard work and dedication, they inspire loyalty and commitment and foster a positive work environment where individuals feel valued and appreciated.

Moreover, leaders inspire trust and respect by being accessible and approachable to their team members. Approachable leaders are willing to listen to their employees' concerns, ideas, and feedback and are responsive to their needs. When leaders are accessible and open to communication, they create an environment where employees feel comfortable sharing their thoughts and opinions. This fosters trust and respect and strengthens the relationship between leaders and their team members.

In conclusion, inspiring trust and respect is essential for achieving a healthy work environment and fostering positive relationships among team members. Effective leaders inspire trust and respect by demonstrating integrity, empathy, transparency, fairness, recognition, and approachability in their actions and interactions with others. By building trust and respect within the workplace, leaders create a supportive and empowering environment where employees feel valued, motivated, and engaged.

Promoting transparency and open communication

Promoting transparency and open communication is integral to achieving a healthy work environment and fostering trust, collaboration, and engagement among employees. Transparency involves sharing relevant information openly and honestly, while open communication encourages dialogue, feedback, and the exchange of ideas within the workplace. When organizations prioritize transparency and open communication, they create a culture of trust, accountability, and mutual respect, which contributes to employee satisfaction, productivity, and overall success.

One of the primary benefits of promoting transparency and open communication is that it fosters trust among employees. When leaders are transparent about organizational goals, decisions, and challenges, employees feel informed and included in the decision-making process. Transparent communication builds credibility and trust, as employees have confidence in the integrity and honesty of their leaders. This trust forms the foundation of a healthy work environment where employees feel valued and respected.

Moreover, promoting transparency and open communication encourages accountability within the organization. When information is shared openly, employees understand their roles and responsibilities and the impact of their actions on the organization's success. This clarity promotes accountability, as employees take ownership of their work and hold themselves and others accountable for their performance and outcomes. Open communication allows for constructive feedback and discussion, which helps identify areas for improvement and fosters a culture of continuous learning and growth.

Furthermore, promoting transparency and open communication enhances collaboration and teamwork within the workplace. When employees have access to information and are encouraged to share their thoughts and ideas openly, they are more likely to collaborate effectively with their colleagues. Open communication facilitates knowledge sharing, problem-solving, and innovation, as employees draw on each other's expertise and perspectives to achieve common goals. Collaboration promotes a sense of belonging and camaraderie among team members, leading to increased engagement and productivity.

Additionally, promoting transparency and open communication contributes to employee satisfaction and retention. When employees feel informed and involved in decision-making processes, they are more likely to feel valued and committed to the organization. Open communication allows employees to voice their opinions and concerns, which helps address issues proactively and prevent misunderstandings or conflicts. Employees who feel heard and respected are more likely to remain loyal to the organization and contribute positively to its success.

Moreover, promoting transparency and open communication strengthens leadership effectiveness within the organization. Leaders who communicate openly and transparently with their teams build trust and credibility, which enhances their ability to influence and inspire others. Transparent communication fosters a culture of transparency and accountability, where leaders lead by example and demonstrate integrity and honesty in their actions. Effective communication skills are essential for leaders to convey their vision, motivate their teams, and drive organizational change and innovation.

In conclusion, promoting transparency and open communication is essential for achieving a healthy work environment and fostering trust, collaboration, and engagement among employees. Transparent communication builds trust, enhances accountability, promotes collaboration, and strengthens leadership effectiveness within the organization. By prioritizing transparency and open communication, organizations can create a culture of transparency, accountability, and mutual respect, where employees feel valued, empowered, and motivated to contribute to the organization's success.

Encouraging teamwork and collaboration

Encouraging teamwork and collaboration is crucial for achieving a healthy work environment and fostering a culture of mutual support, innovation, and success within an organization. Teamwork involves individuals coming together to achieve common goals, while collaboration emphasizes the sharing of knowledge, skills, and resources to accomplish tasks effectively. When organizations prioritize teamwork and collaboration, they create a cohesive and productive work environment where employees feel valued, motivated, and engaged.

One of the primary benefits of encouraging teamwork and collaboration is that it promotes synergy and efficiency in the workplace. When employees work together as a team, they can leverage their diverse skills, perspectives, and experiences to solve problems, make decisions, and achieve objectives more effectively than they could individually. Collaboration enables employees to share knowledge and expertise, leading to better decision-making and innovative solutions. By encouraging teamwork and collaboration, organizations can maximize productivity and achieve better outcomes.

Moreover, encouraging teamwork and collaboration fosters a sense of belonging and camaraderie among employees. When employees collaborate on projects or tasks, they develop strong relationships and bonds with their colleagues. Collaboration promotes open communication, trust, and mutual respect, which are essential for building a positive work environment where individuals feel supported and valued. Employees who feel connected to their team members are more likely to be motivated, engaged, and satisfied with their work.

Furthermore, encouraging teamwork and collaboration promotes learning and development within the organization. When employees collaborate with others, they have the opportunity to learn from their peers, acquire new skills, and broaden their knowledge base. Collaboration also provides a platform for mentoring and coaching, as more experienced employees can share their expertise and insights with others. By fostering a culture of collaboration, organizations can promote continuous learning and growth among their employees, which enhances individual and organizational performance.

Additionally, encouraging teamwork and collaboration enhances innovation and creativity within the organization. When employees from different backgrounds and disciplines come together to collaborate, they bring diverse perspectives and ideas to the table. Collaboration encourages brainstorming, experimentation, and risk-taking, which are essential for generating innovative solutions to complex problems. By fostering a collaborative environment where creativity is valued and encouraged, organizations can drive innovation and stay ahead of the competition.

Moreover, encouraging teamwork and collaboration improves employee engagement and satisfaction. When employees feel included and involved in decision-making processes, they are more likely to be engaged and committed to their work. Collaboration empowers employees to contribute their ideas and opinions, which fosters a sense of ownership and pride in their work. Employees who feel valued and respected for their contributions are more likely to be satisfied with their jobs and remain loyal to the organization.

In conclusion, encouraging teamwork and collaboration is essential for achieving a healthy work environment and fostering a culture of mutual support, innovation, and success within an organization. Teamwork and collaboration promote synergy, efficiency, belonging, learning, development, innovation, and employee engagement. By prioritizing teamwork and collaboration, organizations can create a positive and productive work environment where employees thrive and contribute to the organization's success.

Pacing Work Responsibly

Pacing work responsibly is a crucial aspect of achieving a healthy work environment, as it ensures that employees can maintain productivity and well-being without experiencing burnout or excessive stress. Responsible pacing involves effectively managing workloads, setting realistic deadlines, and prioritizing tasks to maintain a balance between productivity and personal well-being. When employees pace their work responsibly, they can sustain high performance levels while also preserving their physical and mental health.

One of the primary benefits of pacing work responsibly is that it helps prevent burnout among employees. Burnout is a state of physical, emotional, and mental exhaustion caused by prolonged exposure to high levels of stress and workload. By pacing their work responsibly, employees can avoid overexerting themselves and mitigate the risk of burnout. Responsible pacing allows employees to allocate their time and energy effectively, ensuring that they can manage their workload without becoming overwhelmed or fatigued.

Moreover, pacing work responsibly promotes work-life balance, which is essential for employee well-being and satisfaction. Work-life balance involves effectively juggling the demands of work with personal and family responsibilities, hobbies, and self-care activities. When employees pace their work responsibly, they can allocate time for both work and personal life, reducing stress and enhancing overall quality of life. Work-life balance is associated with higher levels of job satisfaction, motivation, and retention, as employees feel more fulfilled and satisfied with their lives.

Furthermore, pacing work responsibly contributes to improved productivity and performance within the organization. When employees manage their workload effectively and avoid overcommitting themselves, they can focus their efforts on high-priority tasks and deliver results more efficiently. Responsible pacing allows employees to work at a sustainable pace, which prevents fatigue and enables them to maintain a high level of performance over the long term. By pacing their work responsibly, employees can achieve better outcomes and contribute to the organization's success.

Additionally, pacing work responsibly promotes better time management and organization skills among employees. When employees pace their work responsibly, they prioritize tasks based on urgency and importance, allocate time for breaks and rest, and set realistic deadlines for completing projects. Responsible pacing requires effective planning and organization, which helps employees manage their time more effectively and meet deadlines consistently. Improved time management skills lead to greater efficiency, reduced stress, and increased productivity in the workplace.

Moreover, pacing work responsibly fosters a culture of trust and respect within the organization. When employees pace their work responsibly, they demonstrate reliability, accountability, and professionalism in their work habits. Responsible pacing involves communicating effectively with supervisors and colleagues about workload, deadlines, and priorities, which promotes transparency and collaboration within the team. By pacing their work responsibly, employees build trust and credibility with their peers and leaders, which enhances teamwork and morale in the workplace.

In conclusion, pacing work responsibly is essential for achieving a healthy work environment and promoting employee well-being, productivity, and satisfaction. Responsible pacing helps prevent burnout, promotes work-life balance, enhances productivity, improves time management skills, and fosters a culture of trust and respect within the organization. By pacing their work responsibly, employees can maintain a sustainable pace, preserve their physical and mental health, and achieve success both personally and professionally.

Recognizing signs of overworking

Recognizing signs of overworking is essential for achieving a healthy work environment and ensuring the well-being of employees. Overworking occurs when individuals consistently work long hours, neglecting breaks, rest, and personal time, which can lead to physical, emotional, and mental exhaustion. By recognizing the signs of overworking, organizations can take proactive measures to support employees, promote work-life balance, and prevent burnout.

One of the key signs of overworking is chronic fatigue and exhaustion. Employees who are overworked often feel constantly tired and depleted, regardless of how much rest they get. They may experience difficulty concentrating, reduced productivity, and increased errors in their work due to fatigue. Chronic fatigue can also manifest as physical symptoms such as headaches, muscle tension, and gastrointestinal issues. Recognizing these signs can help organizations identify employees who may be at risk of burnout and intervene accordingly.

Moreover, overworking can have a significant impact on employees' mental health and well-being. Employees who are overworked may experience heightened levels of stress, anxiety, and irritability due to the pressure to meet deadlines and expectations. They may struggle to switch off from work and experience intrusive thoughts about work-related tasks, even during their personal time. Over time, chronic stress and overworking can contribute to more serious mental health issues such as depression and anxiety disorders. Recognizing these signs allows organizations to provide support and resources for employees to manage their stress and prioritize their well-being.

Additionally, overworking can lead to a decline in job satisfaction and motivation among employees. When individuals consistently work long hours without adequate rest or time for personal activities, they may begin to feel disillusioned and demotivated in their roles. They may lose interest in their work, become disengaged from their tasks, and experience feelings of resentment towards their employers. Recognizing signs of decreased job satisfaction and motivation can help organizations address underlying issues such as workload imbalance and promote a healthier work environment.

Furthermore, overworking can negatively impact employees' relationships and personal lives. Employees who are overworked may struggle to maintain a healthy work-life balance, leading to strained relationships with family and friends. They may miss out on important events and activities due to work commitments, causing feelings of guilt and isolation. Recognizing signs of strained relationships and social withdrawal can help organizations support employees in managing their workload and prioritizing their personal lives.

Moreover, overworking can have long-term consequences for both individuals and organizations. Chronic overwork increases the risk of burnout, which is characterized by emotional exhaustion, depersonalization, and reduced personal accomplishment. Burnout can lead to decreased job performance, increased absenteeism, and higher turnover rates within the organization. Recognizing signs of burnout and overworking allows organizations to implement strategies to address workload issues, promote work-life balance, and support employee well-being.

In conclusion, recognizing signs of overworking is crucial for achieving a healthy work environment and supporting employee well-being. Signs of overworking include chronic fatigue, heightened stress levels, decreased job satisfaction and motivation, strained relationships, and increased risk of burnout. By recognizing these signs, organizations can take proactive measures to address workload issues, promote work-life balance, and create a supportive environment where employees can thrive both personally and professionally.

Implementing sensible working hours

Implementing sensible working hours is a fundamental aspect of achieving a healthy work environment and promoting the well-being of employees. Sensible working hours refer to establishing reasonable limits on the amount of time employees are expected to work each day or week, with the aim of preventing burnout, improving productivity, and enhancing work-life balance. By implementing sensible working hours, organizations can create a culture that prioritizes employee health, happiness, and overall effectiveness.

One of the primary benefits of implementing sensible working hours is the prevention of burnout among employees. Burnout is a state of physical, emotional, and mental exhaustion caused by prolonged exposure to high levels of stress and overwork. By setting sensible limits on working hours, organizations can help employees avoid overexertion and mitigate the risk of burnout. Sensible working hours allow employees to maintain a healthy balance between work and personal life, reducing the likelihood of fatigue and burnout.

Moreover, implementing sensible working hours can lead to improved productivity and performance within the organization. Research has shown that excessive working hours can actually decrease productivity, as fatigue and burnout impair cognitive function, decision-making, and problem-solving abilities. By establishing reasonable limits on working hours, organizations can ensure that employees have adequate time for rest and recovery, leading to increased focus, creativity, and efficiency in their work.

Additionally, implementing sensible working hours promotes better work-life balance among employees. Work-life balance involves effectively managing the demands of work with personal and family responsibilities, hobbies, and self-care activities. Sensible working hours allow employees to allocate time for both work and personal life, reducing stress and improving overall quality of life. Employees who have a healthy work-life balance are more likely to be satisfied with their jobs, experience less stress, and have better physical and mental health.

Furthermore, implementing sensible working hours can lead to reduced absenteeism and turnover rates within the organization. Excessive working hours can contribute to employee fatigue, stress-related illnesses, and dissatisfaction with work, leading to increased absenteeism and turnover. By establishing sensible limits on working hours, organizations can create a more supportive and sustainable work environment, reducing the likelihood of burnout and turnover among employees.

Moreover, implementing sensible working hours can enhance employee morale, motivation, and engagement. When employees feel that their organization values their well-being and respects their time, they are more likely to feel motivated and engaged in their work. Sensible working hours signal to employees that their health and happiness are important priorities for the organization, fostering a sense of loyalty and commitment among the workforce.

In conclusion, implementing sensible working hours is essential for achieving a healthy work environment and promoting the well-being of employees. Sensible working hours help prevent burnout, improve productivity, enhance work-life balance, reduce absenteeism and turnover, and boost employee morale, motivation, and engagement. By prioritizing sensible working hours, organizations can create a culture that supports employee health, happiness, and overall effectiveness, leading to greater success and sustainability in the long term.

Ensuring regular breaks

Ensuring regular breaks is a fundamental component of achieving a healthy work environment and promoting the well-being of employees. Breaks allow employees to rest, recharge, and rejuvenate, which is essential for maintaining productivity, creativity, and overall job satisfaction. By prioritizing regular breaks, organizations can create a culture that values employee health, happiness, and effectiveness.

One of the primary benefits of ensuring regular breaks is the prevention of burnout among employees. Burnout is a state of physical, emotional, and mental exhaustion caused by prolonged exposure to high levels of stress and workload. By encouraging employees to take regular breaks throughout the day, organizations can help prevent fatigue and mitigate the risk of burnout. Breaks provide employees with the opportunity to rest and recharge, allowing them to return to work feeling refreshed and energized.

Moreover, ensuring regular breaks can lead to improved productivity and performance within the organization. Research has shown that taking regular breaks throughout the workday can enhance concentration, focus, and cognitive function. Breaks allow employees to step away from their work tasks momentarily, which can help reduce mental fatigue and improve decision-making and problem-solving abilities. By encouraging regular breaks, organizations can help employees maintain peak performance levels throughout the day.

Additionally, ensuring regular breaks promotes better physical health among employees. Prolonged sitting and sedentary behavior have been linked to a range of health problems, including obesity, cardiovascular disease, and musculoskeletal disorders. By encouraging employees to take regular breaks and move around, organizations can help reduce the negative health effects associated with prolonged sitting. Breaks provide employees with the opportunity to stretch, walk, or engage in other physical activities, which can help improve circulation, reduce muscle tension, and alleviate discomfort.

Furthermore, ensuring regular breaks fosters a positive work culture that values employee well-being and work-life balance. When organizations prioritize regular breaks, they signal to employees that their health and happiness are important priorities. Breaks provide employees with the opportunity to take care of their physical and mental needs, which can help reduce stress and improve overall job satisfaction. Employees who feel supported and valued by their organization are more likely to be engaged, motivated, and loyal to the company.

Moreover, ensuring regular breaks can lead to better collaboration and teamwork within the organization. Breaks provide employees with the opportunity to connect and socialize with their colleagues, which can help strengthen relationships and foster a sense of camaraderie. Additionally, breaks allow employees to step away from their work tasks momentarily, which can help reduce tension and conflict in the workplace. By encouraging regular breaks, organizations can create a more cohesive and supportive work environment where employees feel connected and valued.

In conclusion, ensuring regular breaks is essential for achieving a healthy work environment and promoting the well-being of employees. Regular breaks help prevent burnout, improve productivity, enhance physical health, foster a positive work culture, and promote collaboration and teamwork. By prioritizing regular breaks, organizations can create a supportive and sustainable work environment where employees thrive both personally and professionally.

Respect and Equality in the Workplace

Respect and equality in the workplace are crucial components of achieving a healthy work environment and fostering a positive organizational culture. Respect involves treating all individuals with dignity, courtesy, and consideration, regardless of their position or background, while equality ensures that everyone has fair and equal opportunities for growth, advancement, and recognition. By promoting respect and equality in the workplace, organizations can create a culture that values diversity, promotes inclusion, and supports the well-being and success of all employees.

One of the primary benefits of promoting respect and equality in the workplace is the creation of a positive work culture that values diversity and inclusion. When employees feel respected and valued for their unique perspectives, backgrounds, and contributions, they are more likely to feel engaged, motivated, and committed to their work. Respectful and inclusive workplaces foster a sense of belonging and camaraderie among employees, leading to greater collaboration, teamwork, and innovation.

Moreover, promoting respect and equality in the workplace helps prevent discrimination, harassment, and bias, creating a safe and supportive environment for all employees. Discrimination and harassment based on factors such as race, gender, age, sexual orientation, or disability can have detrimental effects on employee morale, well-being, and productivity. By promoting respect and equality, organizations send a clear message that discriminatory behavior will not be tolerated and that all employees are entitled to fair and equitable treatment.

Additionally, promoting respect and equality in the workplace enhances employee morale, satisfaction, and retention. When employees feel respected and treated fairly, they are more likely to be satisfied with their jobs and committed to the organization. Respectful and inclusive workplaces attract top talent and help retain employees over the long term, reducing turnover and recruitment costs for the organization. Employees who feel valued and respected are also more likely to go above and beyond in their roles, leading to improved performance and productivity.

Furthermore, promoting respect and equality in the workplace enhances teamwork, collaboration, and communication among employees. In environments where respect and equality are prioritized, employees are more likely to listen to and consider the perspectives of others, leading to more effective problem-solving and decision-making.

Respectful and inclusive workplaces foster open dialogue and constructive feedback, allowing employees to share ideas, express concerns, and work together towards common goals.

Moreover, promoting respect and equality in the workplace can have positive effects on the organization's reputation and brand image. Companies that prioritize diversity, inclusion, and respect are viewed more favorably by customers, investors, and the community at large. Respectful and inclusive workplaces demonstrate a commitment to social responsibility and ethical business practices, which can enhance the organization's reputation and attract stakeholders who share similar values.

In conclusion, promoting respect and equality in the workplace is essential for achieving a healthy work environment and fostering a positive organizational culture. Respect and equality create a supportive and inclusive environment where all employees feel valued, respected, and empowered to succeed. By prioritizing respect and equality, organizations can create a culture that promotes diversity, fosters inclusion, and supports the well-being and success of all employees.

Instilling a respect culture

Instilling a culture of respect in the workplace is integral to achieving a healthy work environment and fostering a positive organizational culture. A respect culture emphasizes the importance of treating all individuals with dignity, fairness, and consideration, regardless of their position, background, or beliefs. By instilling a respect culture, organizations can create a work environment where employees feel valued, empowered, and motivated to perform their best.

One of the key benefits of instilling a respect culture is the promotion of trust and collaboration among employees. In a culture of respect, employees feel safe and comfortable expressing their ideas, concerns, and opinions without fear of judgment or reprisal. This open and transparent communication fosters trust and mutual respect among team members, leading to improved collaboration, teamwork, and problem-solving.

Moreover, instilling a respect culture helps prevent conflicts and misunderstandings in the workplace. When employees are treated with respect and consideration, they are less likely to engage in behavior that undermines trust or disrupts harmony within the team. Respectful workplaces encourage constructive dialogue and conflict resolution strategies, allowing employees to address issues and concerns in a timely and professional manner.

Additionally, instilling a respect culture promotes diversity and inclusion within the organization. Respectful workplaces celebrate the unique backgrounds, perspectives, and experiences of all employees, creating a sense of belonging and acceptance for everyone. By valuing diversity and fostering inclusion, organizations can tap into the full potential of their workforce and drive innovation, creativity, and growth.

Furthermore, instilling a respect culture enhances employee morale, satisfaction, and retention. When employees feel respected and valued for their contributions, they are more likely to be engaged and committed to their work. Respectful workplaces attract and retain top talent, reducing turnover and recruitment costs for the organization. Employees who feel appreciated and supported are also more likely to go above and beyond in their roles, leading to improved performance and productivity.

Moreover, instilling a respect culture can have positive effects on the organization's reputation and brand image. Companies that prioritize respect and fairness are viewed more favorably by customers, investors, and the community at large. A reputation for being a respectful and inclusive employer can help attract top talent, strengthen customer loyalty, and enhance the organization's overall competitiveness in the marketplace.

In conclusion, instilling a culture of respect is essential for achieving a healthy work environment and fostering a positive organizational culture. A respect culture promotes trust, collaboration, and inclusion among employees, leading to improved communication, conflict resolution, and teamwork. By valuing diversity and treating all individuals with dignity and fairness, organizations can create a workplace where employees feel respected, valued, and empowered to succeed.

Promoting equality and diversity

Promoting equality and diversity in the workplace is crucial for achieving a healthy work environment and fostering a culture of inclusion, innovation, and collaboration. Equality refers to ensuring that all individuals have equal opportunities, rights, and treatment, regardless of their race, gender, age, sexual orientation, disability, or other characteristics. Diversity encompasses the range of backgrounds, experiences, and perspectives that individuals bring to the workplace. By promoting equality and diversity, organizations can create a work environment where all employees feel valued, respected, and empowered to contribute their unique talents and perspectives.

One of the primary benefits of promoting equality and diversity in the workplace is the creation of a culture of inclusion and belonging. When employees feel that their differences are respected and valued, they are more likely to feel included and accepted within the organization. Inclusive workplaces celebrate diversity and foster a sense of belonging for all employees, regardless of their background or identity. This sense of belonging leads to higher levels of engagement, satisfaction, and retention among employees.

Moreover, promoting equality and diversity in the workplace can lead to improved creativity, innovation, and problem-solving. Diversity of thought and perspective encourages employees to approach challenges from different angles and generate new ideas and solutions. By embracing diverse perspectives, organizations can tap into the full potential of their workforce and drive innovation and growth. Inclusive workplaces also benefit from increased adaptability and resilience, as employees with diverse backgrounds bring a variety of skills and experiences to the table.

Additionally, promoting equality and diversity helps organizations attract and retain top talent. In today's increasingly diverse and globalized world, employees are seeking employers who prioritize diversity, inclusion, and equity. Organizations that demonstrate a commitment to equality and diversity are more likely to attract a diverse pool of candidates and retain top performers. Employees are more likely to stay with organizations where they feel valued, respected, and included, leading to reduced turnover and recruitment costs.

Furthermore, promoting equality and diversity can lead to enhanced customer satisfaction and loyalty. Customers are more likely to trust and support organizations that demonstrate a commitment to diversity, inclusion, and social responsibility. Inclusive workplaces reflect the diversity of their customer base and are better equipped to understand and meet the needs of diverse customer groups. By promoting equality and diversity, organizations can build stronger relationships with customers and enhance their reputation and brand image.

Moreover, promoting equality and diversity in the workplace can have positive effects on society as a whole. Inclusive workplaces serve as role models for other organizations and inspire positive change in the broader community. By championing equality and diversity, organizations can contribute to the creation of a more equitable and inclusive society, where all individuals have equal opportunities to succeed and thrive.

In conclusion, promoting equality and diversity is essential for achieving a healthy work environment and fostering a culture of inclusion, innovation, and collaboration. By embracing diversity and ensuring equal opportunities for all employees, organizations can create a workplace where everyone feels valued, respected, and empowered to succeed. Inclusive workplaces benefit from higher levels of engagement, satisfaction, and retention, as well as improved creativity, innovation, and customer satisfaction. By promoting equality and diversity, organizations can drive positive change within their own walls and in the broader community.

Preventing discrimination and harassment

Preventing discrimination and harassment in the workplace is essential for achieving a healthy work environment where all employees feel safe, respected, and valued. Discrimination and harassment can have serious negative impacts on employee morale, well-being, and productivity, as well as legal and reputational consequences for organizations. By implementing proactive measures to prevent discrimination and harassment, organizations can create a culture of respect, fairness, and inclusivity where employees can thrive.

One of the primary ways to prevent discrimination and harassment is through education and training. Employers should provide comprehensive training programs for employees at all levels to raise awareness about discrimination and harassment, including what constitutes inappropriate behavior and the consequences of engaging in such behavior. Training sessions should cover topics such as unconscious bias, diversity awareness, respectful communication, and bystander intervention techniques. By educating employees about their rights and responsibilities, organizations can empower them to recognize and address discrimination and harassment in the workplace.

Moreover, organizations should establish clear policies and procedures for reporting and addressing instances of discrimination and harassment. These policies should outline the types of behavior that are prohibited, the steps for reporting incidents, the investigation process, and the consequences for offenders. It is essential for organizations to create a safe and confidential reporting process that encourages employees to come forward with concerns without fear of retaliation. By taking reports of discrimination and harassment seriously and conducting prompt and thorough investigations, organizations can demonstrate their commitment to maintaining a respectful and inclusive work environment.

Additionally, organizations should foster a culture of respect and inclusivity by promoting diversity and equity in all aspects of their operations. This includes ensuring equal opportunities for hiring, promotion, and advancement, as well as providing support and accommodations for employees with diverse backgrounds and needs. Employers should strive to create diverse and inclusive teams, foster open dialogue and collaboration, and celebrate the contributions of all employees. By valuing diversity and promoting equity, organizations can create a workplace where everyone feels valued, respected, and empowered to succeed.

Furthermore, leaders and managers play a crucial role in preventing discrimination and harassment in the workplace. It is essential for leaders to set a positive example by modeling respectful behavior and holding themselves and others accountable for upholding organizational values. Leaders should actively listen to employee concerns, address issues promptly and effectively, and provide support and guidance to those who have experienced discrimination or harassment. By demonstrating a commitment to creating a respectful and inclusive work environment, leaders can inspire trust and confidence among employees and help prevent discrimination and harassment from occurring.

Moreover, organizations should regularly assess and evaluate their policies, procedures, and practices to ensure they are effective in preventing discrimination and harassment. This includes conducting regular audits, surveys, and focus groups to gather feedback from employees, identifying areas for improvement, and implementing corrective actions as needed. By continuously monitoring and improving their efforts to prevent discrimination and harassment, organizations can create a workplace where all employees feel safe, respected, and valued.

In conclusion, preventing discrimination and harassment is essential for achieving a healthy work environment where all employees can thrive. By educating employees, establishing clear policies and procedures, promoting diversity and equity, empowering leaders, and continuously monitoring and improving efforts, organizations can create a culture of respect, fairness, and inclusivity where everyone feels valued and respected. By prioritizing prevention efforts, organizations can create a workplace where discrimination and harassment are not tolerated, and all employees can reach their full potential.

Work-Life Balance

Work-life balance has become an increasingly important topic in today's fast-paced work environment, where employees often struggle to juggle the demands of their professional and personal lives. Achieving a healthy work-life balance is essential for maintaining overall well-being, reducing stress, and increasing job satisfaction and productivity. Organizations play a crucial role in promoting work-life balance by implementing policies and practices that support employees in managing their work and personal responsibilities effectively.

One way organizations can support work-life balance is by offering flexible work arrangements. Flexible work options, such as telecommuting, flexible hours, compressed workweeks, and job sharing, allow employees to better accommodate their personal commitments while still meeting their work obligations. Flexibility in work schedules enables employees to better manage their time, reduce commuting stress, and achieve a better balance between work and personal life. Additionally, flexible work arrangements can contribute to higher job satisfaction, increased morale, and improved retention rates among employees.

Furthermore, organizations can encourage employees to take regular breaks and vacations to recharge and rejuvenate. Encouraging employees to use their vacation time and providing opportunities for rest and relaxation helps prevent burnout and promotes overall well-being. Additionally, organizations can implement policies that discourage employees from working long hours or taking work home with them, ensuring that they have time to disconnect and recharge outside of work hours. By prioritizing employee well-being and encouraging a healthy work-life balance, organizations can create a more positive and productive work environment.

Moreover, organizations can provide resources and support for employees to manage their work and personal responsibilities more effectively. This may include offering employee assistance programs, wellness initiatives, and stress management workshops to help employees cope with work-related stress and maintain their overall health and well-being. Additionally, organizations can provide access to resources such as childcare services, eldercare support, and financial counseling to help employees manage their personal obligations more effectively. By providing comprehensive support and resources, organizations can empower employees to achieve a better balance between their work and personal lives.

Additionally, fostering a culture of trust and autonomy can help promote work-life balance among employees. When employees feel trusted and empowered to manage their own workloads and schedules, they are more likely to take ownership of their work and prioritize their personal well-being. By providing autonomy and flexibility in how work is performed, organizations can empower employees to find the right balance between their professional and personal lives. Additionally, recognizing and rewarding employees who prioritize work-life balance can help reinforce a culture that values employee well-being and encourages healthy work-life integration.

Furthermore, organizations can lead by example by promoting work-life balance at all levels of the organization. Senior leaders and managers should prioritize their own work-life balance and encourage employees to do the same. By modeling healthy work-life behaviors and setting realistic expectations for workloads and deadlines, leaders can create a culture that supports work-life balance for all employees. Additionally, leaders should be mindful of the impact their actions and decisions have on employees' work-life balance and take proactive steps to address any issues or concerns that arise.

In conclusion, achieving a healthy work-life balance is essential for employee well-being, job satisfaction, and overall productivity. Organizations can support work-life balance by offering flexible work arrangements, encouraging employees to take regular breaks and vacations, providing resources and support for managing work and personal responsibilities, fostering a culture of trust and autonomy, and leading by example at all levels of the organization. By prioritizing work-life balance, organizations can create a more positive and productive work environment where employees can thrive both personally and professionally.

Importance of work-life balance for employees

Achieving a healthy work-life balance is crucial for employees in maintaining their overall well-being, reducing stress, and improving their quality of life. In today's fast-paced and demanding work environment, where technology allows for constant connectivity and the boundaries between work and personal life can easily blur, prioritizing work-life balance has become increasingly important for employees.

Firstly, maintaining a healthy work-life balance allows employees to take care of their physical and mental health. Long hours and excessive workload can lead to burnout, fatigue, and increased stress levels, which can have negative effects on both physical and mental health. Chronic stress has been linked to a variety of health problems, including cardiovascular disease, depression, and anxiety. By prioritizing work-life balance, employees can better manage their stress levels, get adequate rest, and engage in activities that promote their overall health and well-being.

Moreover, achieving a healthy work-life balance enables employees to spend more time with their families and loved ones, fostering stronger relationships and a greater sense of fulfillment outside of work. Family and personal relationships play a crucial role in an individual's overall happiness and life satisfaction. Spending quality time with family and engaging in activities that bring joy and fulfillment can help employees recharge and rejuvenate, leading to increased job satisfaction and productivity when they return to work.

Additionally, maintaining a healthy work-life balance allows employees to pursue their interests and hobbies outside of work, contributing to their personal growth and fulfillment. Engaging in activities such as hobbies, sports, or volunteering can provide employees with a sense of purpose and fulfillment beyond their professional responsibilities. These activities also serve as outlets for creativity, self-expression, and relaxation, helping employees maintain a healthy work-life balance and overall well-being.

Furthermore, achieving a healthy work-life balance can lead to increased job satisfaction and motivation among employees. When employees feel that they have control over their work schedules and are able to balance their professional and personal responsibilities effectively, they are more likely to feel satisfied with their jobs and committed to their organizations. This, in turn, can lead to higher levels of employee engagement, productivity, and retention, benefiting both employees and employers alike.

Moreover, a healthy work-life balance can improve employees' overall quality of life and happiness. By prioritizing time for leisure, relaxation, and self-care, employees can enjoy a greater sense of fulfillment and satisfaction in all areas of their lives. Achieving a healthy work-life balance allows employees to pursue their passions, cultivate meaningful relationships, and enjoy the simple pleasures of life, leading to a greater sense of overall happiness and well-being.

In conclusion, achieving a healthy work-life balance is essential for employees in maintaining their overall well-being, reducing stress, and improving their quality of life. By prioritizing work-life balance, employees can take care of their physical and mental health, spend quality time with their families and loved ones, pursue their interests and hobbies, increase job satisfaction and motivation, and enjoy a greater sense of overall happiness and fulfillment. Employers play a crucial role in supporting work-life balance by implementing policies and practices that prioritize employee well-being and promote a healthy work-life balance for all employees.

Encouraging timely offs and vacations

Encouraging timely offs and vacations is essential for achieving a healthy work environment that prioritizes employee well-being and productivity. In today's fast-paced work culture, employees often find themselves caught up in the demands of their jobs, neglecting the importance of taking regular breaks and vacations. However, promoting and encouraging timely offs and vacations can have numerous benefits for both employees and organizations.

Firstly, taking regular breaks and vacations allows employees to recharge and rejuvenate, reducing stress and preventing burnout. Continuous work without adequate breaks can lead to increased fatigue, decreased productivity, and overall job dissatisfaction. By encouraging employees to take timely offs and vacations, organizations can help them disconnect from work, relax, and return to their duties with renewed energy and focus. This ultimately leads to higher job satisfaction, increased morale, and improved overall well-being among employees.

Moreover, taking regular breaks and vacations has been shown to improve cognitive function and creativity. Stepping away from work allows employees to clear their minds, gain new perspectives, and generate fresh ideas. Studies have found that individuals who take regular breaks are more productive, creative, and innovative compared to those who work continuously without breaks. Encouraging timely offs and vacations can therefore enhance employee creativity and problem-solving abilities, leading to better outcomes for the organization.

Additionally, taking vacations provides employees with the opportunity to spend quality time with their families and loved ones, strengthening relationships and fostering a greater sense of work-life balance. Family vacations offer employees the chance to create lasting memories, bond with their loved ones, and engage in meaningful experiences outside of work. This helps employees recharge emotionally and return to work feeling more fulfilled and motivated.

Furthermore, taking timely offs and vacations can have positive effects on employee health and well-being. Chronic stress resulting from overwork has been linked to a variety of health problems, including cardiovascular disease, depression, and anxiety. By encouraging employees to take regular breaks and vacations, organizations can help mitigate the negative effects of stress on employee health. Vacations provide employees with the opportunity to rest, relax, and engage in activities that promote physical and mental well-being, such as exercise, meditation, and spending time outdoors.

Moreover, encouraging timely offs and vacations can improve employee retention and loyalty. Employees who feel supported in taking time off are more likely to feel valued and appreciated by their employers. This, in turn, leads to higher levels of job satisfaction and loyalty towards the organization. Employees who are able to maintain a healthy work-life balance are also less likely to experience burnout and turnover, resulting in cost savings for the organization associated with recruitment and training of new employees.

In conclusion, encouraging timely offs and vacations is essential for achieving a healthy work environment that prioritizes employee well-being, productivity, and overall satisfaction. By promoting a culture that values and supports taking breaks and vacations, organizations can reap numerous benefits, including reduced stress and burnout, increased creativity and productivity, improved employee health and well-being, and enhanced retention and loyalty. Employers should therefore take proactive steps to encourage employees to take timely offs and vacations, recognizing the importance of rest and relaxation in maintaining a happy, healthy, and productive workforce.

Setting realistic expectations

Setting realistic expectations is paramount in achieving a healthy work environment that fosters productivity, job satisfaction, and overall well-being among employees. Unrealistic expectations can lead to stress, burnout, and dissatisfaction, ultimately undermining employee morale and productivity. By setting realistic expectations, organizations can create a supportive and sustainable work environment where employees feel valued, motivated, and able to perform at their best.

One aspect of setting realistic expectations involves defining clear and achievable goals and objectives for employees. Clear goals provide employees with a sense of direction and purpose, helping them understand what is expected of them and how their efforts contribute to the organization's success. However, goals that are overly ambitious or unattainable can demotivate employees and lead to feelings of frustration and inadequacy. Therefore, it is essential for organizations to set goals that are challenging yet achievable, taking into account employees' skills, resources, and capabilities.

Furthermore, setting realistic expectations involves providing employees with the necessary resources, support, and guidance to meet their goals. This may include access to training and development opportunities, adequate staffing and equipment, and ongoing feedback and coaching from managers. By ensuring that employees have the tools and support they need to succeed, organizations can increase the likelihood of goal attainment and promote a culture of continuous improvement and growth.

Moreover, setting realistic expectations requires managers to communicate openly and transparently with their teams about workload, priorities, and deadlines. Open communication helps employees understand what is expected of them and allows them to raise any concerns or challenges they may be facing. Managers should work collaboratively with their teams to set realistic timelines and deadlines, taking into account factors such as workload, complexity, and available resources. By involving employees in the goal-setting process and soliciting their input, managers can foster a sense of ownership and accountability, leading to greater commitment and engagement.

Additionally, setting realistic expectations involves recognizing and acknowledging employees' efforts and accomplishments. Positive reinforcement and recognition can boost morale, motivation, and job satisfaction, reinforcing desired behaviors and encouraging continued effort and performance. Managers should celebrate individual and team achievements, whether big or small, and express appreciation for employees' hard work and dedication. Recognizing employees' contributions helps build trust and confidence and fosters a supportive and positive work environment.

Furthermore, setting realistic expectations requires flexibility and adaptability in response to changing circumstances and priorities. Workloads and priorities may shift over time due to factors such as organizational changes, market dynamics, or external events. Therefore, it is important for organizations to be agile and responsive in adjusting expectations and goals as needed. Managers should be willing to reassess priorities, reallocate resources, and revise timelines in order to ensure that expectations remain realistic and achievable in light of changing conditions.

In conclusion, setting realistic expectations is essential for achieving a healthy work environment that promotes employee well-being, productivity, and job satisfaction. By defining clear and achievable goals, providing the necessary resources and support, communicating openly and transparently, recognizing employees' efforts and accomplishments, and remaining flexible and adaptable in response to changing circumstances, organizations can create a supportive and sustainable work environment where employees feel valued, motivated, and able to perform at their best.

Employee Wellness Programs

Employee wellness programs are a crucial component of achieving a healthy work environment that prioritizes the well-being of employees. These programs encompass a variety of initiatives and activities designed to support and promote the physical, mental, and emotional health of employees. From fitness challenges to mental health resources, wellness programs offer employees the tools and support they need to lead healthier and happier lives both inside and outside of the workplace.

One key aspect of employee wellness programs is promoting physical health and fitness. Many programs offer access to gym memberships, fitness classes, or onsite workout facilities to encourage employees to engage in regular exercise and physical activity. Additionally, wellness programs may provide resources and support for healthy eating habits, such as nutrition workshops, cooking demonstrations, or access to healthy snacks and meals in the workplace. By promoting physical health and fitness, employee wellness programs can help reduce the risk of chronic diseases, improve energy levels and productivity, and enhance overall quality of life.

Moreover, employee wellness programs often include initiatives to support mental and emotional well-being. This may involve providing access to mental health resources and support services, such as counseling or therapy sessions, employee assistance programs, or stress management workshops. Additionally, wellness programs may offer mindfulness and meditation sessions, relaxation techniques, or resilience training to help employees cope with stress and improve their mental resilience. By addressing mental health issues and promoting emotional well-being, these programs can help reduce absenteeism, improve job satisfaction, and enhance employee engagement and performance.

Furthermore, employee wellness programs may focus on promoting work-life balance and stress management. This may involve initiatives such as flexible work arrangements, telecommuting options, or policies that encourage employees to take regular breaks and vacations. Additionally, wellness programs may offer resources and support for time management, prioritization, and goal-setting to help employees manage their workload and responsibilities more effectively. By promoting work-life balance and stress management, these programs can help prevent burnout, reduce turnover, and improve overall employee well-being and satisfaction.

In addition to physical and mental health initiatives, employee wellness programs often include initiatives to promote social connectedness and community engagement. This may involve organizing team-building activities, social events, or volunteer opportunities that encourage employees to connect with their colleagues and give back to their communities. By fostering a sense of belonging and camaraderie, these programs can help improve workplace morale, build stronger relationships among employees, and create a more positive and supportive work environment.

Moreover, employee wellness programs may incorporate initiatives to address specific health risks and concerns within the workforce. This may involve conducting health assessments or screenings to identify areas of concern, such as high blood pressure, cholesterol levels, or obesity. Based on the results, wellness programs can then tailor interventions and resources to help employees manage their health risks and improve their overall well-being. By addressing specific health issues and providing targeted support, these programs can help reduce healthcare costs, improve productivity, and enhance employee satisfaction and retention.

In conclusion, employee wellness programs play a vital role in achieving a healthy work environment that supports the well-being of employees. By promoting physical, mental, and emotional health, promoting work-life balance and stress management, fostering social connectedness and community engagement, and addressing specific health risks and concerns, these programs can help create a workplace where employees feel valued, supported, and empowered to thrive both personally and professionally.

Benefits of wellness programs

Wellness programs have become increasingly popular in workplaces across the globe, and for good reason. These programs offer a wide range of benefits for both employees and employers, contributing to the overall goal of achieving a healthy work environment. From improving employee health to increasing productivity and reducing healthcare costs, wellness programs play a crucial role in creating a positive and supportive workplace culture.

One of the primary benefits of wellness programs is the improvement of employee health. By promoting healthy behaviors such as regular exercise, balanced nutrition, and stress management, these programs help employees adopt healthier lifestyles. This, in turn, leads to a reduction in the prevalence of chronic diseases such as obesity, diabetes, and heart disease. Employees who participate in wellness programs are more likely to experience improvements in their overall health, including increased energy levels, better sleep quality, and enhanced physical fitness.

Moreover, wellness programs contribute to increased productivity and performance in the workplace. Healthy employees are more focused, engaged, and motivated to perform their best at work. By supporting employee well-being and addressing factors that can impact productivity, such as stress and fatigue, wellness programs help employees stay mentally sharp and alert throughout the workday. Additionally, initiatives that promote work-life balance and stress management can help prevent burnout and improve job satisfaction, leading to higher levels of productivity and performance.

Furthermore, wellness programs have been shown to reduce healthcare costs for employers. By investing in the health and well-being of their employees, organizations can help prevent costly medical conditions and reduce the frequency of healthcare utilization. Employees who participate in wellness programs are less likely to require medical treatment for preventable conditions, leading to savings in healthcare expenses for employers. Additionally, wellness programs may offer incentives such as reduced insurance premiums or financial rewards for achieving health goals, further incentivizing employees to adopt healthy behaviors and reduce healthcare costs.

In addition to improving physical health and productivity, wellness programs contribute to a positive workplace culture and employee morale. By demonstrating a commitment to employee well-being, employers create a supportive and inclusive work environment where employees feel valued and appreciated. Wellness programs foster a sense of camaraderie and community among employees, as they participate in activities and initiatives together to improve their health and well-being. This sense of belonging and connectedness strengthens relationships among employees and contributes to a more positive and cohesive workplace culture.

Moreover, wellness programs can help attract and retain top talent. In today's competitive job market, prospective employees are increasingly seeking out employers who offer comprehensive wellness programs as part of their benefits package. Organizations that prioritize employee well-being and offer opportunities for personal and professional growth are more likely to attract and retain talented individuals who are committed to their own health and success. By investing in wellness programs, employers demonstrate their commitment to supporting the holistic well-being of their employees, which can have a positive impact on recruitment and retention efforts.

In conclusion, wellness programs offer numerous benefits for both employees and employers, contributing to the achievement of a healthy work environment. From improving employee health and productivity to reducing healthcare costs and fostering a positive workplace culture, these programs play a vital role in supporting the overall well-being and success of employees. By investing in wellness initiatives, organizations can create a workplace where employees thrive personally and professionally, leading to greater satisfaction, engagement, and success for all.

Suggestions for effective programs

Effective wellness programs are essential for achieving a healthy work environment that promotes the well-being and productivity of employees. These programs should be carefully designed to address the unique needs and preferences of employees while aligning with the goals and objectives of the organization. Here are some suggestions for creating effective wellness programs:

Assess Employee Needs: Before implementing a wellness program, it's important to conduct a thorough assessment of employee needs and preferences. This can be done through surveys, focus groups, or interviews to gather feedback and insights from employees about their health and wellness priorities. By understanding the specific needs and interests of employees, organizations can tailor their wellness programs to address the most pressing concerns and interests.

Offer Diverse Wellness Activities: Effective wellness programs should offer a diverse range of activities and initiatives to accommodate the varied interests and preferences of employees. This may include fitness challenges, nutrition workshops, mindfulness sessions, stress management seminars, and team-building activities. By providing a variety of options, employees can choose activities that resonate with them and are more likely to participate and engage in the program.

Provide Educational Resources: Wellness programs should also include educational resources and materials to empower employees with knowledge and information about health and wellness. This may include articles, newsletters, webinars, or online resources about topics such as healthy eating, exercise, mental health, and stress management. By providing educational resources, organizations can help employees make informed decisions about their health and well-being.

Encourage Social Support: Social support is an important aspect of employee wellness, so effective programs should encourage social interaction and support among employees. This can be achieved through team-based challenges, group fitness classes, walking clubs, or wellness committees where employees can connect with each other, share experiences, and provide encouragement and support. By fostering a sense of community and camaraderie, organizations can create a supportive environment where employees feel motivated to pursue their wellness goals together.

Promote Work-Life Balance: Work-life balance is essential for employee well-being, so effective wellness programs should promote initiatives that support work-life balance.

This may include flexible work arrangements, telecommuting options, or policies that encourage employees to take regular breaks and vacations. Additionally, wellness programs can offer resources and support for time management, prioritization, and boundary-setting to help employees manage their workload and personal responsibilities more effectively.

Provide Incentives and Rewards: To incentivize participation and engagement in wellness programs, organizations can offer incentives and rewards for achieving health goals or participating in wellness activities. This may include financial incentives, gift cards, or prizes for reaching milestones such as completing a certain number of workouts, attending wellness workshops, or participating in health screenings. By providing incentives and rewards, organizations can motivate employees to take an active role in their health and well-being.

Measure and Evaluate Program Effectiveness: Finally, it's important to measure and evaluate the effectiveness of wellness programs on an ongoing basis. This can be done through surveys, feedback sessions, or data analysis to assess employee satisfaction, participation rates, health outcomes, and return on investment. By regularly evaluating program effectiveness, organizations can identify areas for improvement and make adjustments to ensure that their wellness programs continue to meet the needs of employees and achieve their intended goals.

In conclusion, effective wellness programs are essential for achieving a healthy work environment that promotes the well-being and productivity of employees. By assessing employee needs, offering diverse wellness activities, providing educational resources, encouraging social support, promoting work-life balance, providing incentives and rewards, and measuring program effectiveness, organizations can create wellness programs that empower employees to live healthier, happier, and more fulfilling lives both inside and outside of the workplace.

Inviting employee participation

Encouraging and inviting employee participation is essential for the success of any wellness program aimed at achieving a healthy work environment. When employees feel empowered and motivated to participate in wellness initiatives, they are more likely to adopt healthy behaviors, engage with the program, and experience positive outcomes. Here are some effective strategies for inviting employee participation in wellness programs:

Create a Culture of Wellness: Cultivating a culture of wellness within the organization is fundamental to inviting employee participation. This involves fostering an environment where health and well-being are valued and prioritized at all levels of the organization. Leaders and managers should lead by example by actively participating in wellness activities and promoting a healthy lifestyle. By demonstrating a commitment to wellness, employees are more likely to feel motivated and encouraged to participate in wellness initiatives.

Communicate Clearly and Effectively: Clear and effective communication is essential for inviting employee participation in wellness programs. Organizations should communicate the purpose, goals, and benefits of the wellness program in a transparent and engaging manner. This may involve using multiple communication channels such as email, newsletters, posters, intranet portals, and staff meetings to keep employees informed and engaged. Providing regular updates and reminders about upcoming wellness activities can help maintain momentum and encourage participation.

Solicit Employee Input and Feedback: Inviting employee input and feedback is crucial for designing wellness programs that resonate with employees' needs and preferences. Organizations should seek input from employees through surveys, focus groups, or suggestion boxes to gather insights about their health and wellness interests, challenges, and goals. By involving employees in the planning and decision-making process, organizations can ensure that wellness initiatives are relevant, meaningful, and appealing to employees.

Offer Choice and Flexibility: Providing employees with choice and flexibility in wellness activities is key to encouraging participation. Wellness programs should offer a variety of activities and initiatives to accommodate diverse interests, preferences, and schedules. This may include options for fitness classes, wellness workshops, mindfulness sessions, and social events that cater to different employee preferences. Additionally, offering flexible participation options such as onsite and virtual activities allows employees to engage in wellness activities in a way that works best for them.

Provide Incentives and Rewards: Incentives and rewards can be powerful motivators for encouraging employee participation in wellness programs. Organizations can offer incentives such as gift cards, prizes, or recognition for achieving health goals, participating in wellness activities, or completing wellness challenges. Additionally, providing rewards for ongoing participation and engagement can help sustain employee interest and motivation over time. By offering meaningful incentives and rewards, organizations can incentivize employees to take an active role in their health and well-being.

Foster Social Support and Accountability: Social support and accountability play a crucial role in motivating employees to participate in wellness programs. Organizations can create opportunities for employees to connect with each other, share experiences, and provide mutual support throughout their wellness journey. This may involve forming wellness committees, buddy systems, or support groups where employees can collaborate, encourage each other, and hold each other accountable for their wellness goals. By fostering a sense of camaraderie and community, organizations can create a supportive environment that motivates employees to participate in wellness activities.

In conclusion, inviting employee participation is essential for the success of wellness programs aimed at achieving a healthy work environment. By creating a culture of wellness, communicating clearly and effectively, soliciting employee input and feedback, offering choice and flexibility, providing incentives and rewards, and fostering social support and accountability, organizations can encourage employees to actively engage in wellness initiatives and reap the benefits of improved health, well-being, and productivity.

Office Space Design and Its Impact

The design of office spaces plays a significant role in shaping the work environment and influencing the well-being and productivity of employees. A well-designed office space can foster collaboration, creativity, and overall job satisfaction, while a poorly designed space can lead to discomfort, stress, and decreased performance. Here's a closer look at the impact of office space design on achieving a healthy work environment:

Physical Comfort: Office space design directly affects the physical comfort of employees, which is essential for their well-being and productivity. Factors such as ergonomic furniture, proper lighting, temperature control, and adequate ventilation contribute to physical comfort in the workplace. Comfortable seating, adjustable desks, and supportive chairs can help prevent musculoskeletal issues and promote good posture, while appropriate lighting and temperature levels can reduce eye strain, fatigue, and discomfort.

Layout and Flow: The layout and flow of an office space can significantly impact employee interaction, communication, and collaboration. Open-plan layouts encourage interaction and collaboration among employees, while private offices offer privacy and concentration for tasks that require focus. Flexible layouts that incorporate both open and private spaces allow employees to choose the environment that best suits their needs, promoting productivity and well-being. Additionally, well-designed circulation paths and clear signage can enhance the flow of traffic and reduce congestion, creating a more efficient and pleasant work environment.

Noise Management: Noise levels in the workplace can have a significant impact on employee well-being and productivity. Excessive noise from nearby workstations, equipment, or common areas can cause distraction, stress, and reduced concentration. Office space design should include measures to manage noise levels, such as sound-absorbing materials, acoustic panels, and strategic placement of workstations. Additionally, designated quiet zones or soundproof rooms can provide employees with opportunities for focused work and concentration, contributing to a healthier and more productive work environment.

Access to Nature: Incorporating elements of nature into office space design, such as natural light, plants, and outdoor views, can have a positive impact on employee well-being and performance. Natural light exposure has been linked to improved mood, energy levels, and sleep quality, while indoor plants can help reduce stress, purify the air, and enhance the overall aesthetic of the workspace. Access to outdoor views and green spaces can also provide opportunities for relaxation and rejuvenation, promoting employee engagement and satisfaction.

Personalization and Flexibility: Office space design should allow for personalization and flexibility to accommodate the diverse needs and preferences of employees. Providing opportunities for personalization, such as adjustable desks, customizable workstations, and designated spaces for personal belongings, empowers employees to create a workspace that reflects their individual preferences and enhances their sense of ownership and well-being. Additionally, flexible workspaces that can be easily reconfigured to support different activities and work styles promote adaptability and creativity, contributing to a healthier and more dynamic work environment.

Psychological Well-being: Office space design can also impact employees' psychological well-being by influencing their sense of autonomy, belonging, and identity in the workplace. A well-designed office space that reflects the values and culture of the organization can foster a sense of pride, belonging, and engagement among employees. Additionally, incorporating elements of biophilic design, such as natural materials, textures, and colors, can evoke feelings of calmness, connection, and inspiration, enhancing employees' overall sense of well-being and satisfaction.

In conclusion, office space design plays a crucial role in achieving a healthy work environment by impacting the physical, social, and psychological well-being of employees. By prioritizing factors such as physical comfort, layout and flow, noise management, access to nature, personalization and flexibility, and psychological well-being, organizations can create office spaces that support employee health, happiness, and productivity.

How architecture affects mood and productivity

Architecture plays a crucial role in shaping our environment, influencing our mood, and impacting productivity. From the design of our homes to the layout of our workplaces, architectural elements have a profound effect on our psychological well-being and overall quality of life. In the context of achieving a healthy work environment, understanding how architecture affects mood and productivity is essential for creating spaces that support employee well-being and enhance performance.

One way architecture influences mood and productivity is through the use of natural light. Exposure to natural light has been shown to have numerous benefits, including boosting mood, enhancing concentration, and regulating the sleep-wake cycle. Buildings with ample windows and skylights allow for increased natural light penetration, creating a brighter and more uplifting environment. Employees working in well-lit spaces tend to feel more alert, focused, and energized, leading to improved productivity and job satisfaction.

In addition to natural light, the layout and spatial configuration of a building can also impact mood and productivity. Open-plan layouts promote communication and collaboration among employees, fostering a sense of community and belonging. However, excessive noise and lack of privacy in open-plan offices can lead to distractions and decreased concentration. On the other hand, private offices or designated quiet areas provide employees with the solitude and focus needed for tasks that require deep concentration. By designing spaces that balance openness with privacy, architects can create environments that support both collaboration and individual productivity.

The choice of materials and textures used in architectural design can also influence mood and productivity. Biophilic design principles emphasize the incorporation of natural elements, such as wood, stone, and greenery, into the built environment. These natural materials have been shown to evoke feelings of calmness, comfort, and connection with nature, which can reduce stress and promote mental well-being. Additionally, incorporating textures and patterns that stimulate the senses, such as soft fabrics or textured surfaces, can create a more engaging and stimulating environment, enhancing creativity and productivity.

Furthermore, the overall aesthetic and atmosphere of a building can impact mood and productivity. Aesthetically pleasing environments with well-designed interiors and thoughtful details can evoke positive emotions and inspire creativity. Conversely, bland or uninspiring spaces may have a negative effect on mood and motivation. By incorporating elements of art, color, and decor that reflect the organization's values and culture, architects can create spaces that foster a sense of identity and pride among employees, leading to greater engagement and productivity.

Another important aspect of architectural design that affects mood and productivity is the integration of green spaces and outdoor environments. Access to nature has been linked to numerous health benefits, including stress reduction, improved cognitive function, and enhanced mood. Incorporating green spaces, such as courtyards, gardens, or rooftop terraces, into the design of buildings provides employees with opportunities for relaxation, recreation, and connection with nature. Additionally, views of natural landscapes or greenery from indoor spaces can have a positive effect on mood and well-being, even if employees are unable to physically access outdoor spaces.

In conclusion, architecture has a significant impact on mood and productivity in the workplace. By considering factors such as natural light, spatial layout, materials and textures, aesthetic appeal, and access to nature, architects can design buildings that promote employee well-being and enhance productivity. Creating environments that support a healthy work-life balance, foster collaboration and creativity, and inspire a sense of connection with the surrounding environment is essential for achieving a healthy work environment and optimizing employee performance.

Enhancing office aesthetics

Enhancing the aesthetics of an office space is crucial for achieving a healthy work environment and fostering employee well-being and productivity. Aesthetics play a significant role in shaping the atmosphere and ambiance of a workplace, influencing the mood, motivation, and satisfaction of employees. By incorporating elements of design that are visually appealing, stimulating, and reflective of the organization's culture, employers can create environments that inspire creativity, collaboration, and a sense of pride among employees.

One way to enhance office aesthetics is through thoughtful interior design. The selection of furniture, color schemes, lighting, and decor can significantly impact the look and feel of a workspace. Choosing ergonomic and stylish furniture not only improves the comfort and functionality of the office but also adds a touch of sophistication and professionalism. Color psychology suggests that certain colors can evoke specific emotions and behaviors. For example, blue is associated with calmness and productivity, while yellow promotes optimism and creativity. Incorporating a variety of colors into the office design can create a dynamic and inspiring environment.

Lighting is another crucial aspect of office aesthetics. Well-designed lighting can enhance the mood, visibility, and overall ambiance of a workspace. Natural light is preferred whenever possible, as it provides numerous health benefits and creates a more inviting and energizing atmosphere. Additionally, incorporating task lighting and ambient lighting can help create different zones within the office, allowing for flexibility and customization based on the needs of employees and activities.

Artwork and decor can also contribute to office aesthetics and employee well-being. Displaying artwork, photographs, or motivational quotes on the walls adds personality and character to the space while stimulating creativity and inspiration. Incorporating plants and greenery into the office design not only improves air quality but also adds a natural and calming element to the environment. Moreover, providing comfortable and inviting breakout areas or lounge spaces encourages relaxation and socialization among employees, fostering a sense of community and belonging.

Furthermore, maintaining a clean and clutter-free workspace is essential for enhancing office aesthetics and promoting productivity. A cluttered and disorganized environment can create feelings of stress, overwhelm, and distraction among employees. Implementing effective storage solutions, such as filing cabinets, shelves, and organizational systems, helps keep the workspace neat and orderly. Encouraging employees to declutter their desks and common areas regularly promotes a sense of cleanliness and orderliness, contributing to a more visually pleasing and harmonious work environment.

In addition to physical elements, incorporating branding and company culture into office aesthetics is essential for creating a sense of identity and pride among employees. Displaying the company logo, mission statement, and core values prominently throughout the office reinforces the organization's identity and cultivates a sense of belonging among employees. Moreover, incorporating elements of the company's culture, such as artwork, signage, and branded merchandise, reinforces the company's values and fosters a sense of community and camaraderie among employees.

In conclusion, enhancing office aesthetics is essential for achieving a healthy work environment and promoting employee well-being and productivity. By incorporating elements of design that are visually appealing, stimulating, and reflective of the organization's culture, employers can create environments that inspire creativity, collaboration, and a sense of pride among employees. From interior design and lighting to artwork and branding, every aspect of office aesthetics plays a role in shaping the atmosphere and ambiance of the workspace.

Achieving a comfortable workspace

Creating a comfortable workspace is essential for achieving a healthy work environment and promoting employee well-being and productivity. A comfortable workspace not only enhances physical comfort but also contributes to mental and emotional well-being, leading to increased job satisfaction and performance. There are several key factors to consider when designing and organizing a workspace to ensure maximum comfort for employees.

One important aspect of achieving a comfortable workspace is providing ergonomic furniture and equipment. Ergonomic chairs with adjustable height, lumbar support, and armrests help maintain proper posture and reduce the risk of musculoskeletal injuries such as back pain and neck strain. Similarly, ergonomic desks that can be adjusted to the appropriate height and angle allow employees to work comfortably and efficiently. Providing ergonomic accessories such as keyboard trays, footrests, and monitor stands further enhances comfort and reduces the risk of repetitive strain injuries.

In addition to ergonomic furniture, it's essential to consider the layout and organization of the workspace. Cluttered and cramped environments can contribute to feelings of stress and discomfort, while well-organized and spacious layouts promote a sense of openness and ease. Providing adequate space between workstations allows for freedom of movement and reduces feelings of claustrophobia. Moreover, arranging furniture and equipment in a way that maximizes natural light and minimizes glare helps create a pleasant and visually comfortable environment.

Another crucial aspect of achieving a comfortable workspace is maintaining optimal temperature and air quality. Extremes in temperature, whether too hot or too cold, can negatively impact employee comfort and productivity. Maintaining a consistent temperature within the recommended range, typically between 68-76°F (20-24°C), ensures that employees can work comfortably without feeling too hot or too cold. Additionally, ensuring proper ventilation and air circulation helps maintain indoor air quality, reducing the risk of airborne pollutants and promoting a healthier and more comfortable workspace.

Furthermore, providing amenities such as adjustable lighting and noise control measures can contribute to a more comfortable work environment. Adjustable lighting allows employees to customize the brightness and color temperature of their workspace according to their preferences and tasks. Additionally, implementing sound-absorbing materials and soundproofing measures helps reduce distractions and create a quieter and more conducive work environment.

Creating designated relaxation and break areas within the workspace is also important for promoting comfort and well-being. Providing comfortable seating, soft lighting, and amenities such as coffee machines or water coolers allows employees to take short breaks and recharge throughout the day. Encouraging employees to take regular breaks and providing opportunities for relaxation helps prevent burnout and promotes overall well-being.

Moreover, fostering a culture of flexibility and autonomy contributes to a more comfortable and empowering work environment. Allowing employees to personalize their workspace with personal items and decor creates a sense of ownership and belonging. Additionally, offering flexible work arrangements such as remote work options or flexible hours gives employees greater control over their work-life balance and promotes a more comfortable and accommodating work environment.

In conclusion, achieving a comfortable workspace is essential for creating a healthy work environment and promoting employee well-being and productivity. By providing ergonomic furniture and equipment, optimizing layout and organization, maintaining optimal temperature and air quality, and offering amenities and opportunities for relaxation, employers can create a workspace that prioritizes employee comfort and supports overall well-being. Creating a comfortable workspace not only enhances physical comfort but also contributes to mental and emotional well-being, leading to increased job satisfaction and performance.

Encouraging Skill Development

Encouraging skill development among employees is crucial for achieving a healthy work environment and fostering continuous growth and innovation within organizations. By investing in the professional development of employees, employers can cultivate a culture of learning, empowerment, and adaptability, which contributes to overall job satisfaction and organizational success.

One way to encourage skill development is by providing opportunities for training and development programs. Offering workshops, seminars, webinars, and online courses on topics relevant to employees' roles and career aspirations allows them to acquire new skills, knowledge, and competencies. These programs not only enhance employees' capabilities but also demonstrate the organization's commitment to their growth and development.

Additionally, creating mentorship and coaching programs facilitates knowledge sharing and skill transfer among employees. Pairing junior employees with experienced mentors or coaches provides them with valuable guidance, feedback, and support as they navigate their career paths. Moreover, reverse mentoring programs, where younger employees mentor senior leaders on topics such as technology or diversity, promote cross-generational learning and collaboration.

Encouraging employees to pursue certifications and credentials related to their field of expertise is another effective way to promote skill development. Supporting employees financially or through paid study leave to obtain industry-recognized certifications not only enhances their professional credentials but also demonstrates the organization's investment in their career advancement.

Furthermore, providing opportunities for cross-functional collaboration and project-based learning allows employees to gain exposure to different areas of the organization and develop a diverse skill set. Assigning employees to cross-departmental projects or task forces encourages collaboration, teamwork, and knowledge exchange, fostering a culture of innovation and continuous improvement.

Moreover, fostering a culture of feedback and recognition is essential for promoting skill development and growth. Providing constructive feedback and recognition for achievements and contributions helps employees identify areas for improvement and build upon their strengths. Regular performance reviews and development conversations enable employees to set goals, track progress, and receive support and guidance from their managers.

Encouraging a growth mindset among employees is also essential for promoting skill development and resilience in the face of challenges. Encouraging employees to embrace challenges, learn from failures, and seek opportunities for growth fosters a culture of continuous learning and improvement. Celebrating and rewarding experimentation and innovation encourages employees to take risks and explore new ideas and approaches.

Furthermore, creating a supportive and inclusive work environment is crucial for fostering skill development and employee engagement. Providing equal access to learning and development opportunities for all employees, regardless of their background or level within the organization, promotes diversity and inclusion and ensures that everyone has the chance to reach their full potential.

In conclusion, encouraging skill development among employees is essential for achieving a healthy work environment and driving organizational success. By investing in training and development programs, creating mentorship and coaching opportunities, supporting employees' pursuit of certifications, fostering cross-functional collaboration, providing feedback and recognition, promoting a growth mindset, and creating a supportive and inclusive work environment, employers can empower employees to thrive and contribute to the success of the organization. Encouraging skill development not only enhances employees' capabilities and job satisfaction but also strengthens the organization's competitive advantage and ability to adapt to change.

Fostering talent and potential

Fostering talent and potential within the workplace is essential for achieving a healthy work environment and maximizing the contribution of employees to organizational success. By nurturing talent and recognizing the potential of employees, organizations can create a culture of empowerment, engagement, and excellence.

One way to foster talent and potential is by implementing talent development programs. These programs identify high-potential employees and provide them with opportunities for growth, development, and advancement within the organization. By offering leadership development programs, mentorship opportunities, and stretch assignments, organizations can nurture the skills and capabilities of talented individuals, preparing them for future leadership roles and responsibilities.

Moreover, providing regular feedback and coaching to employees is crucial for fostering talent and potential. By offering constructive feedback, guidance, and support, managers can help employees identify their strengths and areas for improvement and develop the skills needed to excel in their roles. Coaching sessions allow employees to set goals, track progress, and receive personalized support and development opportunities tailored to their individual needs and aspirations.

Creating a culture of continuous learning and innovation is also essential for fostering talent and potential. By encouraging employees to seek out new challenges, take risks, and embrace opportunities for growth, organizations can stimulate creativity, ingenuity, and adaptability. Providing access to learning resources, such as training programs, workshops, and online courses, empowers employees to expand their knowledge and skills and unlock their full potential.

Furthermore, recognizing and celebrating the achievements and contributions of employees is crucial for fostering talent and potential. By acknowledging employees' accomplishments, organizations demonstrate their appreciation for their hard work and dedication and motivate them to continue striving for excellence. Recognizing talent through awards, recognition programs, and public praise not only boosts morale but also inspires other employees to reach their full potential.

Promoting diversity and inclusion is another key aspect of fostering talent and potential within the workplace. By embracing diversity of thought, background, and perspective, organizations can tap into a wide range of talents and ideas, driving innovation and creativity. Creating an inclusive work environment where all employees feel valued, respected, and empowered to contribute enables organizations to attract and retain top talent from diverse backgrounds and experiences.

Moreover, providing opportunities for career development and advancement is essential for fostering talent and potential. By offering clear career paths, promotional opportunities, and professional growth opportunities, organizations can inspire employees to invest in their long-term career development and contribute their skills and talents to the organization's success. Offering mentorship programs, networking opportunities, and career coaching services helps employees navigate their career paths and realize their full potential.

In conclusion, fostering talent and potential within the workplace is essential for achieving a healthy work environment and maximizing organizational success. By implementing talent development programs, providing feedback and coaching, creating a culture of continuous learning and innovation, recognizing and celebrating achievements, promoting diversity and inclusion, and offering opportunities for career development and advancement, organizations can empower employees to thrive and reach their full potential. Fostering talent not only enhances employee engagement and satisfaction but also strengthens the organization's competitive advantage and ability to adapt to change.

Importance of continued learning

Continued learning plays a pivotal role in achieving a healthy work environment and fostering individual and organizational growth. In today's rapidly evolving world, where technological advancements and market dynamics are constantly changing, the importance of ongoing learning cannot be overstated. Here, we delve into the significance of continued learning and its impact on achieving a thriving workplace environment.

Firstly, continued learning enhances employee engagement and satisfaction. When employees are provided with opportunities for professional development and skill enhancement, they feel valued and motivated. Engaged employees are more likely to be invested in their work, leading to increased productivity, higher job satisfaction, and reduced turnover rates. By promoting a culture of learning, organizations can cultivate a workforce that is enthusiastic about their roles and committed to achieving common goals.

Moreover, continued learning fosters innovation and creativity within the workplace. As employees acquire new knowledge and skills, they are better equipped to think critically, solve complex problems, and generate innovative ideas. Continuous learning encourages employees to challenge the status quo, explore new possibilities, and adapt to changing circumstances. By encouraging a culture of innovation, organizations can stay ahead of the curve and remain competitive in the market.

Furthermore, continued learning helps employees stay abreast of industry trends and best practices. In today's knowledge-based economy, staying relevant is crucial for individual and organizational success. By investing in ongoing training and development programs, organizations can ensure that their employees possess the latest skills and knowledge required to excel in their roles. This not only enhances employee performance but also strengthens the organization's position in the market.

Continued learning also promotes personal and professional growth. By acquiring new skills and expanding their knowledge base, employees can unlock new opportunities for career advancement and progression. Ongoing learning allows individuals to broaden their horizons, explore new career paths, and pursue their aspirations. Organizations that prioritize employee development are more likely to attract and retain top talent, as employees are drawn to opportunities for growth and advancement.

Furthermore, continued learning fosters a culture of adaptability and resilience within the workplace. In today's fast-paced business environment, change is inevitable. By equipping employees with the skills and knowledge needed to adapt to change, organizations can navigate challenges more effectively and seize opportunities for growth. Continuous learning encourages employees to embrace change, learn from experiences, and evolve with the evolving needs of the business.

Additionally, continued learning promotes diversity and inclusion within the workplace. By providing equal access to learning opportunities for all employees, organizations can foster a culture of diversity and inclusion. When employees from diverse backgrounds have access to ongoing training and development programs, they are better able to contribute their unique perspectives and talents to the organization. This not only enriches the workplace culture but also enhances creativity, innovation, and problem-solving.

In conclusion, continued learning is essential for achieving a healthy work environment and driving individual and organizational success. By promoting employee engagement, fostering innovation, staying abreast of industry trends, supporting personal and professional growth, cultivating adaptability, and promoting diversity and inclusion, organizations can create a workplace where employees thrive. Continued learning is not only beneficial for employees but also essential for the long-term sustainability and competitiveness of organizations in today's dynamic business landscape.

Implementing practical training

Implementing practical training programs is a crucial component of achieving a healthy work environment and fostering individual and organizational growth. Practical training equips employees with the hands-on skills and knowledge needed to excel in their roles, enhances job performance, and promotes a culture of continuous learning and improvement. Here, we explore the significance of implementing practical training and its impact on creating a thriving workplace environment.

Practical training programs provide employees with the opportunity to acquire job-specific skills and competencies that are directly applicable to their roles. By offering hands-on training sessions, workshops, and simulations, organizations can ensure that employees have the practical skills needed to perform their duties effectively and efficiently. Practical training allows employees to gain valuable experience and confidence in executing tasks, leading to increased productivity and job satisfaction.

Moreover, practical training promotes employee engagement and motivation. When employees are actively involved in hands-on learning activities, they are more likely to be engaged and attentive. Practical training sessions provide employees with a sense of ownership and accountability for their learning, leading to greater enthusiasm and commitment to applying new skills on the job. Engaged employees are more likely to contribute their best efforts and become valuable assets to the organization.

Furthermore, practical training fosters a culture of continuous improvement within the workplace. By regularly updating and enhancing training programs to reflect changing industry trends and best practices, organizations can ensure that employees stay current and competitive. Practical training encourages employees to seek out opportunities for growth and development, driving innovation and excellence within the organization. Continuous improvement initiatives supported by practical training programs enable organizations to adapt to evolving market demands and maintain a competitive edge.

Practical training also enhances teamwork and collaboration within the workplace. By providing employees with opportunities to work together on practical exercises and projects, organizations can foster a sense of camaraderie and mutual support. Practical training encourages employees to share knowledge, skills, and best practices with their colleagues, leading to stronger bonds and improved teamwork. Collaboration promoted by practical training programs enables employees to leverage each other's strengths and expertise, resulting in better problem-solving and decision-making outcomes.

Moreover, practical training helps organizations address skills gaps and talent shortages. By identifying areas where employees lack proficiency or expertise, organizations can tailor practical training programs to address specific needs and requirements. Practical training enables employees to acquire new skills and competencies that are aligned with organizational goals and objectives, ensuring that the workforce remains capable and adaptable in the face of changing demands.

In conclusion, implementing practical training programs is essential for achieving a healthy work environment and driving individual and organizational success. Practical training equips employees with job-specific skills, enhances engagement and motivation, fosters a culture of continuous improvement, promotes teamwork and collaboration, and addresses skills gaps and talent shortages. By investing in practical training initiatives, organizations can empower their employees to excel in their roles, contribute to organizational growth, and thrive in today's dynamic business environment.

Feedback and Recognition

Feedback and recognition are essential components of achieving a healthy work environment and fostering employee engagement, motivation, and productivity. They play a crucial role in providing employees with valuable insights into their performance, reinforcing positive behaviors, and acknowledging their contributions to the organization. Here, we explore the significance of feedback and recognition and their impact on creating a thriving workplace environment.

Feedback is a powerful tool for helping employees understand their strengths and areas for improvement. Constructive feedback provides employees with specific, actionable insights into their performance, helping them identify areas where they excel and areas where they can grow. By offering regular feedback, managers can guide employees towards achieving their full potential and meeting organizational goals. Feedback also facilitates open communication and dialogue between employees and managers, fostering trust, transparency, and collaboration within the workplace.

Moreover, feedback promotes a culture of continuous learning and development. When employees receive timely and relevant feedback on their work, they are better equipped to make informed decisions, improve their skills, and enhance their performance. Feedback encourages employees to reflect on their actions, seek out opportunities for growth, and take ownership of their development. By providing ongoing feedback, organizations can empower their employees to take charge of their career paths and achieve their professional aspirations.

In addition to feedback, recognition is equally important for creating a positive work environment. Recognition acknowledges employees' efforts, accomplishments, and contributions to the organization, reinforcing positive behaviors and fostering a sense of appreciation and belonging. Recognizing employees for their hard work and dedication boosts morale, motivation, and job satisfaction, leading to increased engagement and productivity. Whether through formal awards, public praise, or simple expressions of gratitude, recognition reinforces the organization's values and reinforces a culture of appreciation and respect.

Furthermore, recognition promotes employee retention and loyalty. Employees who feel valued and appreciated are more likely to remain committed to their organization and go above and beyond to contribute to its success. Recognizing employees for their achievements and milestones strengthens the bond between employees and the organization, reducing turnover rates and enhancing employee loyalty. Recognition also serves as a powerful motivator for employees to continue striving for excellence and making meaningful contributions to the organization's objectives.

Additionally, feedback and recognition contribute to a positive work culture characterized by trust, respect, and collaboration. When employees receive regular feedback and recognition from their managers and peers, they feel valued and respected, fostering a sense of camaraderie and teamwork within the workplace. A culture that prioritizes feedback and recognition encourages employees to support each other, celebrate successes, and collaborate on shared goals, leading to a more cohesive and harmonious work environment.

In conclusion, feedback and recognition are integral components of achieving a healthy work environment and promoting employee engagement, motivation, and productivity. Feedback provides employees with valuable insights into their performance and opportunities for growth, while recognition acknowledges their contributions and reinforces positive behaviors. By prioritizing feedback and recognition, organizations can create a workplace culture characterized by trust, respect, and collaboration, where employees feel valued, appreciated, and empowered to succeed.

Creating a culture of regular feedback

Creating a culture of regular feedback is vital for achieving a healthy work environment and promoting continuous improvement, employee development, and organizational success. Regular feedback facilitates open communication, fosters trust, and empowers employees to excel in their roles. Here, we delve into the significance of establishing a culture of regular feedback and its impact on cultivating a thriving workplace environment.

Regular feedback fosters a culture of continuous learning and improvement within the organization. When feedback is provided on a regular basis, employees receive timely insights into their performance, enabling them to identify areas for growth and development. By offering ongoing feedback, managers can guide employees in refining their skills, addressing performance gaps, and achieving their full potential. A culture of regular feedback encourages employees to embrace feedback as an opportunity for learning and personal growth, leading to increased engagement and job satisfaction.

Moreover, regular feedback promotes transparency and accountability in the workplace. When feedback is consistently communicated to employees, it creates a culture of trust and openness, where employees feel comfortable sharing their thoughts, concerns, and ideas. Transparent communication fosters a sense of accountability, as employees understand the expectations and standards set for them and are accountable for their performance. In addition, regular feedback helps mitigate misunderstandings and conflicts by providing clarity and alignment on expectations and goals.

Furthermore, regular feedback strengthens the manager-employee relationship. When managers regularly engage in feedback conversations with their employees, it builds rapport, trust, and mutual respect. Employees feel valued and supported when their managers take an active interest in their development and provide constructive feedback to help them succeed. Stronger manager-employee relationships lead to better communication, increased loyalty, and higher levels of employee engagement.

Additionally, regular feedback drives performance and productivity. By providing employees with ongoing feedback on their performance, managers can identify areas of strength and areas for improvement, enabling employees to perform at their best. Regular feedback helps employees stay focused, motivated, and aligned with organizational goals, leading to improved performance outcomes and increased productivity. Employees who receive regular feedback are more likely to take initiative, set goals, and strive for excellence in their work.

Furthermore, regular feedback fosters a culture of recognition and appreciation. In addition to providing constructive feedback, managers should also recognize and acknowledge employees for their contributions and achievements. Regular feedback sessions present opportunities to celebrate successes, highlight accomplishments, and express gratitude for a job well done. Recognition reinforces positive behaviors, boosts morale, and encourages employees to continue performing at a high level.

In conclusion, creating a culture of regular feedback is essential for achieving a healthy work environment and driving organizational success. Regular feedback promotes continuous learning, transparency, accountability, and trust within the organization. It strengthens manager-employee relationships, drives performance and productivity, and fosters a culture of recognition and appreciation. By prioritizing regular feedback, organizations can empower their employees to reach their full potential, contribute to the organization's goals, and thrive in today's dynamic work environment.

Recognizing employee accomplishments

Recognizing employee accomplishments is a crucial aspect of achieving a healthy work environment and fostering a culture of appreciation, motivation, and engagement. When employees' efforts and achievements are acknowledged and celebrated, it not only boosts morale and job satisfaction but also reinforces positive behaviors and promotes a sense of belonging within the organization. Here, we explore the significance of recognizing employee accomplishments and its impact on creating a positive workplace environment.

First and foremost, recognizing employee accomplishments demonstrates appreciation and gratitude for their hard work and dedication. Employees who feel valued and appreciated are more likely to be engaged, motivated, and committed to their work. By acknowledging their contributions and successes, organizations can cultivate a culture of appreciation, where employees feel recognized and respected for their efforts. This, in turn, fosters a positive work environment where employees are motivated to perform at their best and contribute to the organization's success.

Moreover, recognizing employee accomplishments strengthens employee morale and job satisfaction. When employees receive recognition for their achievements, it validates their efforts and instills a sense of pride and accomplishment. Recognition boosts morale by affirming employees' contributions and reinforcing their sense of purpose and value within the organization. Employees who feel appreciated and valued are more likely to experience higher levels of job satisfaction and are motivated to continue making meaningful contributions to the organization.

Furthermore, recognizing employee accomplishments reinforces positive behaviors and encourages employees to strive for excellence. When employees see their efforts being acknowledged and rewarded, it serves as a powerful motivator to continue performing at a high level. Recognition reinforces behaviors that align with the organization's values and goals, such as teamwork, innovation, and customer service excellence. By recognizing and rewarding exemplary performance, organizations can inspire other employees to emulate these behaviors and contribute to a culture of continuous improvement and success.

In addition, recognizing employee accomplishments promotes a sense of belonging and camaraderie within the organization. When employees receive recognition for their achievements, it fosters a sense of connection and camaraderie among team members.

Recognition events and ceremonies provide opportunities for employees to come together, celebrate their successes, and build stronger relationships with their colleagues. This sense of belonging enhances teamwork, collaboration, and mutual support within the organization, leading to a more cohesive and united workforce.

Furthermore, recognizing employee accomplishments can have a positive impact on employee retention and loyalty. Employees who feel recognized and appreciated are more likely to stay committed to their organization and are less likely to seek opportunities elsewhere. Recognition reinforces employees' sense of loyalty to the organization and strengthens their emotional attachment to their work and colleagues. By recognizing employee accomplishments, organizations can increase employee retention rates, reduce turnover costs, and maintain a talented and engaged workforce.

In conclusion, recognizing employee accomplishments is essential for achieving a healthy work environment and promoting employee engagement, morale, and productivity. Recognition demonstrates appreciation for employees' efforts and contributions, boosts morale and job satisfaction, reinforces positive behaviors, fosters a sense of belonging and camaraderie, and enhances employee retention and loyalty. By prioritizing employee recognition, organizations can create a positive workplace culture where employees feel valued, motivated, and empowered to succeed.

How to give positive and constructive feedback

Giving positive and constructive feedback is an essential skill for leaders and managers in creating a healthy work environment where employees feel supported, motivated, and empowered to succeed. When feedback is delivered effectively, it can inspire growth, development, and improvement while fostering trust, communication, and collaboration within the organization. Here, we explore strategies for giving positive and constructive feedback that promotes a positive work environment and enhances employee performance and engagement.

Firstly, it is crucial to focus on the positive aspects of the employee's performance before addressing areas for improvement. Start by highlighting the employee's strengths, accomplishments, and contributions. Positive feedback acknowledges the employee's efforts and achievements, reinforces their confidence, and motivates them to continue performing at their best. By recognizing and appreciating what the employee is doing well, you create a supportive and encouraging atmosphere that encourages growth and development.

Additionally, when providing constructive feedback, it is important to be specific, objective, and actionable. Focus on the behavior or outcome that needs improvement rather than criticizing the individual. Provide specific examples of the employee's actions or behaviors and how they have impacted their performance or the team's goals. Avoid generalizations or personal attacks, and instead, offer constructive suggestions for improvement that are clear, achievable, and relevant to the employee's role and responsibilities.

Furthermore, feedback should be delivered in a timely manner to be most effective. Address issues or concerns as soon as they arise to prevent them from escalating and to provide the employee with an opportunity to course-correct in a timely manner. Delayed feedback can lead to frustration, confusion, and missed opportunities for growth and improvement. By providing timely feedback, you demonstrate your commitment to the employee's success and show that you are invested in helping them reach their full potential.

Moreover, feedback should be delivered in a respectful and empathetic manner, taking into account the employee's feelings, perspectives, and concerns. Approach the conversation with empathy and understanding, and strive to maintain a positive and supportive tone throughout the discussion. Be mindful of your language and body language, and avoid using accusatory or confrontational language that may cause the employee to become defensive or disengaged. Instead, focus on fostering open and honest communication, and encourage the employee to share their thoughts, ideas, and perspectives.

Additionally, it is important to follow up on feedback and provide ongoing support and guidance to help the employee succeed. Check in regularly to see how the employee is progressing and offer additional support or resources as needed. Recognize and celebrate improvements and milestones along the way, and continue to provide feedback and guidance to ensure continued growth and development.

In conclusion, giving positive and constructive feedback is essential for creating a healthy work environment where employees feel valued, supported, and empowered to succeed. By focusing on the positive aspects of the employee's performance, providing specific and actionable feedback, delivering feedback in a timely and respectful manner, and following up on feedback with ongoing support and guidance, leaders and managers can foster a culture of continuous improvement, collaboration, and success within the organization.

Handling Conflict

Conflict in the workplace is inevitable, but how it is managed can significantly impact the overall health and productivity of an organization. Effectively handling conflict is essential for achieving a healthy work environment where employees feel respected, heard, and supported. Here, we explore strategies for handling conflict in the workplace to promote positive relationships, open communication, and collaborative problem-solving.

Firstly, it is important to address conflict proactively rather than allowing it to escalate. Encourage open communication and create opportunities for employees to voice their concerns, opinions, and perspectives. Establish clear channels for resolving conflicts, such as regular team meetings, one-on-one discussions, or mediation sessions. By addressing conflicts early on, you can prevent them from escalating and minimize their impact on productivity and morale.

Additionally, it is essential to listen actively and empathetically to all parties involved in the conflict. Encourage employees to express their thoughts and feelings without interruption and demonstrate empathy and understanding. By actively listening to each other, employees can gain a better understanding of the underlying issues and work together to find mutually beneficial solutions. Avoid making assumptions or jumping to conclusions, and instead, seek clarification and ask open-ended questions to facilitate dialogue and understanding.

Furthermore, when addressing conflicts, focus on the issues at hand rather than personal attacks or blame. Encourage employees to discuss their concerns and perspectives objectively and respectfully. Avoid getting caught up in emotions or past grievances and instead, focus on finding solutions that address the underlying issues and meet the needs of all parties involved. By keeping the conversation focused on the issues, you can promote constructive dialogue and collaboration.

Moreover, it is important to encourage compromise and collaboration when resolving conflicts. Encourage employees to work together to find win-win solutions that address the needs and interests of all parties involved. Foster a culture of collaboration and teamwork where employees feel empowered to work together to overcome challenges and achieve common goals. By promoting collaboration, you can turn conflicts into opportunities for growth, learning, and innovation.

Additionally, it is essential to provide support and guidance to employees involved in conflicts. Offer coaching, mentoring, or training to help employees develop conflict resolution skills and strategies. Provide resources and tools, such as conflict resolution workshops or mediation services, to help employees effectively manage conflicts and resolve differences constructively. By providing support and guidance, you can empower employees to handle conflicts confidently and professionally.

In conclusion, handling conflict effectively is essential for achieving a healthy work environment where employees feel valued, respected, and supported. By addressing conflicts proactively, listening actively and empathetically, focusing on the issues at hand, encouraging compromise and collaboration, and providing support and guidance to employees, leaders and managers can create a culture of open communication, trust, and respect within the organization. By promoting constructive conflict resolution, organizations can foster positive relationships, enhance productivity, and create a more positive and inclusive work environment for all employees.

Pre-emptively addressing potential conflicts

Preemptively addressing potential conflicts in the workplace is crucial for fostering a healthy work environment where employees feel supported, respected, and motivated. By identifying and addressing potential sources of conflict before they escalate, organizations can proactively prevent misunderstandings, reduce tension, and promote positive relationships among team members.

One effective strategy for preemptively addressing potential conflicts is to establish clear expectations and guidelines for communication and behavior. Clearly define roles, responsibilities, and performance expectations for all employees, and communicate these expectations regularly through team meetings, employee handbooks, or performance evaluations. By setting clear expectations, organizations can minimize ambiguity and reduce the likelihood of misunderstandings or conflicts arising due to differing interpretations of roles or responsibilities.

Additionally, fostering a culture of open communication and transparency can help preemptively address potential conflicts. Encourage employees to voice their concerns, opinions, and ideas openly and respectfully, and provide opportunities for feedback and dialogue. Create channels for employees to communicate with each other and with management, such as suggestion boxes, anonymous feedback surveys, or regular check-in meetings. By promoting open communication, organizations can address issues early on and prevent them from escalating into conflicts.

Furthermore, promoting diversity and inclusion in the workplace can help preemptively address potential conflicts related to discrimination or bias. Embrace diversity and create a culture of inclusivity where employees feel valued and respected regardless of their background, identity, or beliefs. Implement diversity training programs to raise awareness of unconscious biases and promote understanding and appreciation of different perspectives. By fostering a diverse and inclusive workplace, organizations can prevent conflicts related to discrimination or bias and create a more positive and supportive work environment for all employees.

Moreover, providing conflict resolution training and resources to employees can help preemptively address potential conflicts by equipping them with the skills and strategies needed to resolve disputes effectively. Offer workshops or seminars on topics such as communication skills, negotiation techniques, and conflict resolution strategies. Provide access to mediation services or conflict resolution experts who can help facilitate productive dialogue and resolve conflicts before they escalate. By investing in conflict resolution training and resources, organizations can empower employees to address conflicts proactively and constructively.

Additionally, implementing regular team-building activities and fostering a sense of camaraderie among employees can help preemptively address potential conflicts by strengthening relationships and promoting teamwork. Organize team-building exercises, social events, or volunteer opportunities that encourage collaboration, communication, and mutual respect among team members. By fostering a positive and supportive team environment, organizations can prevent conflicts by building strong bonds and fostering a sense of belonging among employees.

In conclusion, preemptively addressing potential conflicts is essential for achieving a healthy work environment where employees feel valued, respected, and motivated. By establishing clear expectations and guidelines, promoting open communication and transparency, embracing diversity and inclusion, providing conflict resolution training and resources, and fostering strong relationships among team members, organizations can proactively prevent conflicts and create a positive and supportive workplace culture. By addressing potential sources of conflict before they escalate, organizations can promote productivity, teamwork, and employee satisfaction, ultimately contributing to their overall success and well-being.

Fairly resolving disputes

Fairly resolving disputes in the workplace is paramount for cultivating a healthy work environment where employees feel heard, respected, and valued. Disputes and conflicts are inevitable in any workplace, but how they are managed can significantly impact the overall morale, productivity, and satisfaction of employees. Employers must adopt effective strategies and processes to address disputes promptly and fairly to maintain a positive work culture and minimize negative consequences.

One crucial aspect of fairly resolving disputes is establishing clear policies and procedures for addressing conflicts. Employers should have well-defined protocols in place outlining how disputes will be handled, including the steps to take, the individuals involved, and the timeline for resolution. By providing clear guidelines, employees know what to expect and can navigate conflicts more effectively, reducing the likelihood of disputes escalating into larger issues.

Additionally, employers must ensure that disputes are addressed promptly and impartially. All parties involved should have the opportunity to express their concerns and perspectives in a safe and supportive environment. Employers should designate impartial mediators or HR professionals to facilitate discussions and help find mutually acceptable resolutions. By remaining neutral and objective, mediators can promote fairness and encourage collaboration in resolving disputes.

Furthermore, employers should encourage open communication and dialogue between conflicting parties. Effective communication is essential for understanding each other's viewpoints, identifying underlying issues, and finding common ground. Employers can facilitate discussions through mediation sessions, team meetings, or one-on-one conversations, providing a platform for employees to express themselves constructively and work towards resolution.

Moreover, it is essential to address disputes with empathy and understanding. Recognizing the emotions involved and acknowledging the impact of the conflict on individuals can help foster empathy and compassion among employees. Employers should encourage empathy by listening actively, showing empathy towards all parties, and validating their feelings and experiences. By acknowledging emotions and demonstrating empathy, employers can create a supportive environment where employees feel heard and valued, enhancing the likelihood of a successful resolution.

Additionally, employers should focus on finding win-win solutions that address the needs and interests of all parties involved. Rather than imposing unilateral decisions or compromises, employers should work collaboratively with employees to find solutions that are acceptable to everyone. This may involve brainstorming alternative options, exploring creative solutions, or seeking outside perspectives. By prioritizing collaboration and cooperation, employers can foster a sense of ownership and commitment among employees towards resolving disputes.

Furthermore, employers should provide training and resources to employees on conflict resolution skills and techniques. Investing in employee development can empower individuals to handle conflicts more effectively and proactively. Training programs on topics such as communication, negotiation, and problem-solving can equip employees with the tools and strategies needed to address disputes confidently and constructively. By investing in employee training, employers can build a more resilient and conflict-competent workforce capable of navigating disputes with professionalism and integrity.

In conclusion, fairly resolving disputes is essential for achieving a healthy work environment where employees feel respected, valued, and supported. Employers can achieve this by establishing clear policies and procedures, addressing conflicts promptly and impartially, promoting open communication and dialogue, demonstrating empathy and understanding, seeking win-win solutions, and providing training and resources to employees. By adopting these strategies, employers can create a positive work culture that fosters collaboration, trust, and mutual respect, ultimately enhancing employee morale, productivity, and satisfaction.

Promoting reconciliation and cooperation

Promoting reconciliation and cooperation in the workplace is crucial for achieving a healthy work environment characterized by mutual respect, trust, and productivity. Conflict and disagreements are inevitable in any workplace setting, but how organizations handle these situations can significantly impact employee morale, job satisfaction, and overall productivity. Employers must prioritize strategies that foster reconciliation and cooperation among employees to create a harmonious and supportive work environment.

One effective way to promote reconciliation and cooperation is through fostering open communication channels. Encouraging employees to express their concerns, opinions, and perspectives in a respectful and constructive manner creates an environment where conflicts can be addressed openly and transparently. Employers can facilitate communication by organizing regular team meetings, one-on-one discussions, or anonymous feedback systems, allowing employees to voice their grievances and work towards resolution collaboratively.

Additionally, promoting reconciliation and cooperation requires cultivating a culture of empathy and understanding within the workplace. Employers should encourage employees to empathize with their colleagues' perspectives and experiences, acknowledging the diverse backgrounds and viewpoints present in the workforce. By fostering empathy, employees can better understand each other's motivations and intentions, paving the way for reconciliation and cooperation.

Moreover, employers should provide opportunities for employees to engage in conflict resolution training and workshops. These programs can equip employees with the necessary skills and techniques to navigate conflicts effectively and promote reconciliation and cooperation. Training sessions may cover topics such as active listening, conflict resolution strategies, and negotiation skills, empowering employees to address disagreements constructively and collaboratively.

Furthermore, promoting reconciliation and cooperation involves encouraging forgiveness and letting go of past grievances. Employers should emphasize the importance of moving forward and focusing on finding solutions rather than dwelling on past conflicts. Encouraging employees to forgive and extend grace to their colleagues fosters a culture of forgiveness and understanding, enabling individuals to work together towards common goals.

Additionally, employers can facilitate team-building activities and initiatives to strengthen relationships among employees and promote cooperation. Team-building exercises, retreats, and social events provide opportunities for employees to bond, build trust, and develop a sense of camaraderie. By fostering positive relationships and interpersonal connections, employers can create a supportive and collaborative work environment conducive to reconciliation and cooperation.

Moreover, employers should lead by example and demonstrate a commitment to reconciliation and cooperation in their own interactions and decision-making processes. By modeling positive behavior and communication, leaders can set the tone for the entire organization and inspire employees to emulate similar attitudes and behaviors. Leaders should prioritize transparency, inclusivity, and fairness in their actions, promoting a culture of mutual respect and cooperation among employees.

In conclusion, promoting reconciliation and cooperation is essential for achieving a healthy work environment characterized by trust, respect, and productivity. Employers can promote reconciliation and cooperation by fostering open communication channels, cultivating empathy and understanding, providing conflict resolution training, encouraging forgiveness, facilitating team-building activities, and leading by example. By prioritizing these strategies, organizations can create a supportive and collaborative work environment where employees feel valued, respected, and motivated to succeed.

Workplace Policies and Rules

Workplace policies and rules play a crucial role in achieving a healthy work environment by providing structure, guidance, and standards for behavior and performance. These policies are essential for promoting fairness, safety, and productivity within the organization. By establishing clear and transparent guidelines, employers can create a positive work culture where employees feel respected, supported, and empowered to succeed.

One of the key aspects of workplace policies is ensuring compliance with legal regulations and industry standards. Employers are responsible for implementing policies that adhere to local, state, and federal laws, as well as industry-specific regulations. These policies may include guidelines for equal employment opportunity, anti-discrimination, workplace safety, and ethical conduct. By prioritizing legal compliance, employers can protect the rights and well-being of their employees while minimizing legal risks for the organization.

Moreover, workplace policies serve to promote fairness and equality among employees by establishing consistent standards for behavior and performance. Policies related to recruitment, hiring, promotions, and compensation ensure that decisions are based on merit, qualifications, and job performance rather than personal biases or preferences. Additionally, policies prohibiting harassment, discrimination, and retaliation create a safe and inclusive work environment where all employees are treated with dignity and respect.

Furthermore, workplace policies contribute to promoting employee well-being and work-life balance. Policies related to flexible work arrangements, telecommuting, and leave benefits allow employees to manage their work responsibilities while accommodating personal and family commitments. By offering flexibility and support, employers can enhance employee satisfaction, morale, and retention rates, leading to a healthier and more engaged workforce.

Additionally, workplace policies play a vital role in promoting professionalism and ethical conduct among employees. Policies outlining expected behaviors, dress codes, and use of company resources ensure that employees adhere to high standards of professionalism and integrity in their interactions with colleagues, clients, and stakeholders. Moreover, policies related to confidentiality, data security, and conflict of interest help protect sensitive information and maintain the trust and reputation of the organization.

Furthermore, workplace policies contribute to promoting a safe and healthy work environment by addressing health and safety concerns. Policies related to workplace ergonomics, accident prevention, and emergency procedures ensure that employees are provided with a safe and conducive work environment. Additionally, policies promoting health and wellness initiatives, such as wellness programs, smoking cessation programs, and mental health support services, encourage employees to prioritize their physical and mental well-being.

Moreover, workplace policies play a crucial role in managing performance and addressing issues of misconduct or poor performance. Performance management policies outline expectations, goals, and evaluation criteria for employees, providing them with clear feedback and guidance on their performance. Additionally, disciplinary policies establish procedures for addressing instances of misconduct or performance deficiencies, ensuring that corrective actions are taken promptly and consistently.

In conclusion, workplace policies and rules are essential for achieving a healthy work environment by providing structure, guidance, and standards for behavior and performance. These policies contribute to promoting fairness, equality, professionalism, safety, and employee well-being within the organization. By prioritizing the development and implementation of effective workplace policies, employers can create a positive and supportive work culture where employees feel valued, respected, and motivated to succeed.

Instituting sensible and clear rules

Establishing sensible and clear rules is fundamental to fostering a healthy work environment that promotes productivity, collaboration, and employee well-being. These rules serve as guidelines for behavior, communication, and performance expectations within the organization, contributing to a harmonious and efficient workplace culture.

Sensible rules are those that are practical, fair, and relevant to the needs of the organization and its employees. They should be based on logical reasoning and aimed at achieving specific objectives, such as ensuring safety, maintaining productivity, and upholding organizational values. Sensible rules take into account the unique circumstances and challenges faced by the organization and its workforce, adapting to changing conditions and needs over time.

Moreover, clear rules are essential for ensuring understanding, compliance, and accountability among employees. Clear rules are written in a concise and easily understandable manner, free from ambiguity or confusion. They outline expectations, responsibilities, and consequences in a straightforward manner, leaving no room for interpretation or misinterpretation. Clear rules provide employees with clarity and guidance on how to conduct themselves and perform their duties effectively within the organization.

Instituting sensible and clear rules begins with identifying the specific needs and objectives of the organization. Employers should assess the unique characteristics, goals, and challenges of their workplace to determine the most relevant and effective rules to implement. This process may involve consulting with employees, conducting surveys or assessments, and seeking input from relevant stakeholders to ensure that the rules reflect the values and priorities of the organization.

Once the rules are identified, it is essential to communicate them effectively to all employees. Clear and transparent communication is key to ensuring that employees understand the rules, their rationale, and the expectations associated with them. Employers should provide comprehensive training and orientation sessions to educate employees about the rules and their implications. Additionally, written documentation, such as employee handbooks or policy manuals, should be made available to employees for reference.

Furthermore, it is important to establish mechanisms for enforcing and monitoring compliance with the rules. Employers should develop procedures for addressing violations or infractions of the rules, ensuring that corrective actions are taken promptly and consistently. This may involve implementing disciplinary measures, providing coaching or feedback, or offering additional training or support as needed. By holding employees accountable for their actions and behaviors, employers can maintain a culture of respect, fairness, and accountability in the workplace.

Additionally, employers should regularly review and update the rules to ensure that they remain relevant, effective, and aligned with the goals and values of the organization. As the business environment evolves and changes, rules may need to be adjusted or modified to address new challenges or opportunities. Employers should seek feedback from employees, monitor compliance and effectiveness, and make adjustments as necessary to ensure that the rules continue to support a healthy and productive work environment.

In conclusion, instituting sensible and clear rules is essential for achieving a healthy work environment that promotes productivity, collaboration, and employee well-being. Sensible rules are practical and relevant to the needs of the organization, while clear rules are easily understandable and free from ambiguity. By identifying specific objectives, communicating effectively, enforcing compliance, and regularly reviewing and updating the rules, employers can create a culture of respect, fairness, and accountability that fosters success and satisfaction among employees.

Enforcing policies justly

Enforcing policies justly is a critical component of achieving a healthy work environment where employees feel valued, respected, and supported. Just enforcement of policies ensures fairness, equity, and consistency in how rules and regulations are applied across the organization, contributing to a positive workplace culture and employee morale.

One of the key principles of enforcing policies justly is treating all employees with fairness and impartiality. Regardless of their position, tenure, or relationship with management, employees should be held to the same standards and expectations outlined in the organization's policies and procedures. This means that disciplinary actions or consequences should be applied consistently and without bias, based solely on the merits of each individual case.

Moreover, just enforcement of policies requires clear communication and transparency about the expectations and consequences associated with non-compliance. Employees should be made aware of the rules, regulations, and expectations governing their conduct and performance within the organization. This includes providing access to written policies and procedures, conducting training sessions or orientations, and offering opportunities for clarification or discussion as needed.

Furthermore, enforcing policies justly involves providing employees with due process and procedural fairness when addressing alleged violations or misconduct. This includes providing employees with the opportunity to present their side of the story, gather evidence or witnesses in their defense, and participate in a fair and impartial review process. Employers should ensure that disciplinary actions are based on objective evidence and are proportionate to the severity of the offense.

In addition to procedural fairness, employers should consider the individual circumstances and mitigating factors surrounding each case when enforcing policies. This may include taking into account factors such as the employee's past performance, disciplinary history, personal circumstances, and intent when determining appropriate sanctions or corrective actions. By considering these factors, employers can ensure that disciplinary decisions are reasonable, compassionate, and supportive of employee growth and development.

Furthermore, it is essential to provide ongoing support and resources to employees to help them understand and comply with organizational policies and procedures. This may include offering training and development opportunities, providing access to counseling or support services, and fostering a culture of open communication and feedback. By investing in the professional and personal development of employees, employers can help prevent policy violations and promote a culture of respect, accountability, and integrity in the workplace.

Moreover, employers should regularly review and evaluate their policies and enforcement practices to ensure that they remain relevant, effective, and aligned with the organization's goals and values. This may involve soliciting feedback from employees, conducting surveys or assessments, and benchmarking against industry best practices. By continuously monitoring and improving policies and enforcement practices, employers can create a supportive and inclusive work environment where employees feel valued, respected, and empowered to succeed.

In conclusion, enforcing policies justly is essential for achieving a healthy work environment that promotes fairness, equity, and employee well-being. By treating all employees with fairness and impartiality, providing clear communication and procedural fairness, considering individual circumstances and mitigating factors, offering ongoing support and resources, and regularly reviewing and evaluating policies and practices, employers can create a culture of trust, respect, and accountability that fosters success and satisfaction among employees.

Regularly reviewing and updating policies

Regularly reviewing and updating policies is a crucial aspect of achieving a healthy work environment that promotes productivity, morale, and compliance. In today's rapidly evolving business landscape, organizations must adapt their policies to address changing legal requirements, industry standards, and internal needs. By regularly reviewing and updating policies, employers can ensure that their workplace remains fair, safe, and supportive for all employees.

One of the primary reasons for regularly reviewing and updating policies is to ensure compliance with relevant laws, regulations, and industry standards. Employment laws and regulations are subject to frequent changes at the federal, state, and local levels, and organizations must stay abreast of these developments to avoid legal liabilities and penalties. By reviewing policies regularly, employers can identify any outdated or non-compliant provisions and make necessary updates to ensure legal compliance.

Moreover, regular policy reviews enable organizations to address emerging issues, trends, and best practices within their industry. As businesses evolve and new challenges arise, policies may need to be revised or expanded to address these changes effectively. For example, advancements in technology may necessitate updates to data security and privacy policies, while shifts in workplace demographics may require revisions to diversity and inclusion policies.

Furthermore, regular policy reviews provide an opportunity for employers to gather feedback from employees and stakeholders about the effectiveness and relevance of existing policies. Employee input can help identify areas where policies may be unclear, inconsistent, or outdated, as well as opportunities for improvement or enhancement. By soliciting feedback from employees, employers can ensure that policies reflect the needs, values, and expectations of the workforce.

In addition to legal compliance and industry standards, regular policy reviews help organizations maintain alignment with their mission, vision, and values. As companies grow and evolve, their strategic priorities and organizational culture may change, requiring updates to policies to reflect these shifts. By ensuring that policies are aligned with the organization's goals and values, employers can foster a culture of accountability, integrity, and transparency in the workplace.

Moreover, regular policy reviews help organizations identify and address potential risks and liabilities before they escalate into larger problems. By proactively reviewing policies for gaps, inconsistencies, or areas of concern, employers can take corrective action to mitigate risks and prevent costly legal disputes or reputational damage. This proactive approach to risk management helps protect both employees and the organization as a whole.

Additionally, regular policy reviews provide an opportunity for employers to communicate updates and changes effectively to employees. Clear and timely communication about policy changes helps ensure that employees understand their rights, responsibilities, and expectations within the organization. Employers can use various communication channels, such as employee handbooks, intranet portals, and training sessions, to disseminate information about policy updates and revisions.

In conclusion, regularly reviewing and updating policies is essential for achieving a healthy work environment that promotes compliance, alignment, and risk management. By staying informed about legal requirements and industry standards, gathering feedback from employees, maintaining alignment with organizational goals and values, proactively addressing risks, and communicating changes effectively, employers can create a workplace where employees feel supported, respected, and empowered to succeed.

Effective Communication

Effective communication is the cornerstone of achieving a healthy work environment that fosters collaboration, productivity, and employee satisfaction. In today's fast-paced and interconnected world, organizations rely on clear and transparent communication to convey information, coordinate activities, and build relationships among employees. By prioritizing effective communication strategies, employers can create a workplace where employees feel valued, informed, and engaged.

One of the key aspects of effective communication in the workplace is clarity. Clear communication ensures that messages are easily understood and interpreted by employees, minimizing the risk of confusion or misunderstandings. Employers can achieve clarity by using simple and concise language, avoiding jargon or technical terms, and providing context or examples when necessary. By communicating clearly, employers can enhance employee comprehension and minimize errors or misinterpretations.

Moreover, effective communication involves active listening and feedback. Employers should create opportunities for employees to express their thoughts, concerns, and ideas openly, and actively listen to their input without judgment or interruption. By soliciting feedback from employees and incorporating their perspectives into decision-making processes, employers can foster a culture of inclusivity, trust, and mutual respect in the workplace. Additionally, providing constructive feedback to employees helps them understand their performance expectations and areas for improvement, ultimately contributing to their professional development and growth.

Furthermore, effective communication requires transparency and honesty. Employers should strive to be open and transparent about organizational goals, priorities, and challenges, and provide regular updates and updates on relevant developments. By keeping employees informed about changes or developments that may affect their work or well-being, employers can build trust and confidence in leadership and demonstrate a commitment to transparency and accountability. Additionally, honesty in communication helps maintain credibility and integrity within the organization, fostering a culture of honesty and ethical behavior.

Additionally, effective communication involves choosing the right communication channels and mediums. In today's digital age, organizations have access to a wide range of communication tools and technologies, including email, instant messaging, video conferencing, and collaboration platforms. Employers should select the most appropriate communication channels for conveying different types of information and messages, taking into account factors such as urgency, complexity, and audience preferences. By choosing the right communication channels, employers can ensure that messages reach the intended recipients in a timely and efficient manner, enhancing overall communication effectiveness.

Moreover, effective communication encompasses cultural sensitivity and inclusivity. In diverse workplaces, employees may come from different cultural backgrounds, languages, and communication styles. Employers should be mindful of cultural differences and adapt their communication strategies accordingly to ensure that messages are inclusive, respectful, and accessible to all employees. By embracing diversity and cultural sensitivity in communication, employers can create a more inclusive and harmonious work environment where all employees feel valued and respected.

In conclusion, effective communication is essential for achieving a healthy work environment characterized by collaboration, productivity, and employee satisfaction. By prioritizing clarity, active listening, transparency, honesty, appropriate communication channels, and cultural sensitivity, employers can foster a workplace culture that values communication and empowers employees to succeed. Effective communication not only enhances organizational performance but also strengthens relationships and fosters a sense of belonging and engagement among employees.

Facilitating open dialogue

Facilitating open dialogue is crucial for achieving a healthy work environment that encourages transparency, collaboration, and mutual respect among employees. Open dialogue refers to the free exchange of ideas, feedback, and concerns among individuals within an organization, fostering a culture of communication and trust. By promoting open dialogue, employers can create a workplace where employees feel empowered to voice their opinions, contribute to decision-making processes, and address issues constructively.

One of the primary benefits of facilitating open dialogue in the workplace is improved communication. When employees are encouraged to communicate openly and honestly with each other and with their supervisors, it creates a culture of transparency and trust. Open dialogue enables employees to share their thoughts, ideas, and concerns freely, leading to better collaboration, problem-solving, and decision-making. Moreover, by promoting open dialogue, employers can identify and address issues or challenges in a timely manner, preventing potential conflicts or misunderstandings from escalating.

Furthermore, open dialogue promotes employee engagement and empowerment. When employees feel that their voices are heard and valued, they are more likely to be engaged in their work and committed to the organization's goals. By creating opportunities for open dialogue, employers can empower employees to take ownership of their work, contribute to organizational success, and actively participate in initiatives aimed at improving the workplace. Moreover, open dialogue fosters a sense of inclusivity and belonging, as employees from diverse backgrounds and perspectives are encouraged to participate and share their unique insights.

Additionally, open dialogue fosters a culture of innovation and creativity. When employees feel comfortable expressing their ideas and opinions without fear of judgment or reprisal, it creates a fertile environment for innovation and creativity to flourish. Open dialogue encourages brainstorming, experimentation, and the exchange of ideas, leading to new insights, solutions, and opportunities for improvement. Moreover, by soliciting input from employees at all levels of the organization, employers can harness the collective wisdom and creativity of their workforce to drive innovation and stay ahead of the competition.

Moreover, open dialogue contributes to employee well-being and satisfaction. When employees feel that their voices are heard and their concerns are taken seriously, it enhances their sense of psychological safety and job satisfaction. Open dialogue enables employees to express their needs and preferences, seek support when needed, and collaborate with colleagues to find solutions to work-related challenges. Moreover, by promoting open dialogue, employers demonstrate a commitment to creating a supportive and inclusive work environment where employees feel valued, respected, and supported in their professional and personal growth.

In conclusion, facilitating open dialogue is essential for achieving a healthy work environment characterized by transparency, collaboration, and mutual respect. Open dialogue promotes improved communication, employee engagement, empowerment, innovation, and well-being. By creating a culture of open dialogue, employers can foster a workplace where employees feel heard, valued, and empowered to contribute to organizational success. Moreover, open dialogue enables organizations to leverage the diverse perspectives and talents of their workforce to drive innovation, creativity, and continuous improvement. Ultimately, open dialogue is a cornerstone of a healthy work environment where employees thrive and organizations succeed.

Addressing communication barriers

Addressing communication barriers is vital for fostering a healthy work environment where employees can collaborate effectively, resolve conflicts, and achieve common goals. Communication barriers can impede the flow of information, lead to misunderstandings, and hinder productivity. By identifying and addressing these barriers, employers can create a workplace culture that promotes clear, open, and effective communication among team members.

One common communication barrier in the workplace is a lack of clarity or ambiguity in messages. When communication is unclear or ambiguous, it can lead to misunderstandings, confusion, and errors. To address this barrier, employers can encourage employees to communicate clearly and concisely, using language that is easy to understand and free of jargon. Additionally, providing context and background information can help ensure that messages are interpreted correctly and that all relevant information is conveyed.

Another common communication barrier is poor listening skills. Effective communication is a two-way process that involves both speaking and listening. When employees are not actively listening to each other, it can result in miscommunication and frustration. To overcome this barrier, employers can promote active listening skills among employees, such as maintaining eye contact, asking clarifying questions, and paraphrasing what was said to ensure understanding. Additionally, creating a culture of respect and empathy can encourage employees to listen attentively to each other's perspectives and concerns.

Cultural and language differences can also pose significant communication barriers in diverse workplaces. Different cultural backgrounds, communication styles, and language proficiency levels can lead to misunderstandings and misinterpretations. To address this barrier, employers can provide cross-cultural communication training to employees, helping them understand and appreciate cultural differences and learn effective strategies for communicating across cultures. Providing language interpretation services and translated materials can also help ensure that all employees have access to important information and can participate fully in workplace communication.

Technological barriers, such as reliance on email or digital communication tools, can also hinder effective communication in the workplace. While technology can enhance communication and collaboration, it can also create barriers when overused or mismanaged. To overcome this barrier, employers can encourage face-to-face communication whenever possible, especially for complex or sensitive topics. Additionally, providing training and support on how to use digital communication tools effectively can help employees navigate technological barriers and communicate more efficiently.

Hierarchical barriers, such as power differentials or organizational silos, can also impede communication in the workplace. When employees feel intimidated or hesitant to communicate with supervisors or colleagues in higher positions, it can lead to a lack of transparency and collaboration. To address this barrier, employers can create a culture of open communication and approachability, where all employees feel comfortable expressing their ideas, concerns, and feedback. Implementing regular check-ins, team meetings, and opportunities for cross-functional collaboration can help break down hierarchical barriers and foster a culture of inclusivity and collaboration.

In conclusion, addressing communication barriers is essential for achieving a healthy work environment where employees can communicate effectively, collaborate productively, and achieve common goals. By identifying and addressing common communication barriers, such as lack of clarity, poor listening skills, cultural differences, technological challenges, and hierarchical barriers, employers can create a workplace culture that promotes clear, open, and respectful communication among team members. Ultimately, effective communication is a cornerstone of a healthy work environment where employees feel valued, engaged, and empowered to contribute to organizational success.

Improving listening skills

Improving listening skills is crucial for fostering a healthy work environment where effective communication, collaboration, and mutual understanding thrive. Listening is an essential component of communication, and individuals who possess strong listening skills are better equipped to build positive relationships, resolve conflicts, and contribute to organizational success. By enhancing listening skills, employees can create a more inclusive, supportive, and productive work environment.

One key aspect of improving listening skills is practicing active listening. Active listening involves fully concentrating on what the speaker is saying, without interrupting or formulating a response prematurely. Instead of simply hearing the words spoken, active listeners focus on understanding the speaker's message, emotions, and underlying concerns. To practice active listening, employees can maintain eye contact, nod in acknowledgment, and provide verbal and nonverbal cues to indicate understanding and engagement.

Additionally, paraphrasing and summarizing the speaker's message can help demonstrate active listening and ensure that both parties are on the same page. By restating the speaker's main points in their own words, listeners can clarify any misunderstandings and confirm their understanding of the message. This reflective listening technique not only enhances comprehension but also shows respect for the speaker's perspective and fosters trust and rapport.

Another effective way to improve listening skills is to minimize distractions and give the speaker undivided attention. In today's fast-paced work environment, distractions such as smartphones, email notifications, and background noise can hinder effective listening. To overcome these distractions, employees can create a conducive listening environment by silencing electronic devices, finding a quiet space for discussions, and practicing mindfulness techniques to stay present and focused.

Empathy is also a critical component of effective listening. Empathetic listeners strive to understand the speaker's feelings, perspectives, and experiences, even if they disagree with them. By putting themselves in the speaker's shoes and showing genuine concern and compassion, empathetic listeners create a safe and supportive space for open communication and emotional expression. Empathy strengthens interpersonal relationships, builds trust, and fosters a sense of belonging in the workplace.

Feedback plays a vital role in improving listening skills. Receiving constructive feedback from colleagues, supervisors, or professional development programs can help individuals identify areas for improvement and refine their listening skills. By soliciting feedback from others and reflecting on their communication behaviors, employees can continuously enhance their listening skills and adapt to different communication styles and preferences.

Training and development opportunities are also valuable resources for improving listening skills in the workplace. Employers can offer workshops, seminars, or online courses on active listening techniques, conflict resolution strategies, and emotional intelligence to help employees enhance their communication skills. By investing in employee development, organizations demonstrate their commitment to fostering a healthy work environment where effective communication and collaboration are prioritized.

In conclusion, improving listening skills is essential for achieving a healthy work environment characterized by open communication, mutual respect, and teamwork. By practicing active listening, minimizing distractions, showing empathy, seeking feedback, and investing in training and development, employees can enhance their listening skills and contribute to a positive and productive workplace culture. Ultimately, effective listening is a foundational skill that empowers individuals to build strong relationships, resolve conflicts, and achieve shared goals in the workplace.

Mental Health Support At Work

Creating a workplace environment that prioritizes mental health support is essential for achieving overall employee well-being and productivity. When employees feel supported and valued in terms of their mental health, they are more likely to thrive in their roles and contribute positively to the organization. In this regard, various strategies and initiatives can be implemented to ensure that mental health support is readily available and accessible to all employees.

One effective approach to promoting mental health support at work is by offering employee assistance programs (EAPs). EAPs typically provide confidential counseling services, resources, and referrals to help employees manage a wide range of personal and work-related issues, including stress, anxiety, depression, substance abuse, and relationship problems. By offering EAPs, employers demonstrate their commitment to supporting employees' mental health and well-being, while also addressing any potential barriers to seeking help.

Another important aspect of mental health support at work is raising awareness and reducing stigma surrounding mental health issues. Employers can organize educational workshops, seminars, or training sessions to increase understanding and awareness of mental health conditions, symptoms, and available resources. By fostering an open and supportive culture where employees feel comfortable discussing mental health concerns without fear of judgment or discrimination, organizations can help break down barriers to seeking help and encourage early intervention.

Moreover, providing flexible work arrangements can significantly contribute to supporting employees' mental health. Flexible work options, such as remote work, flexible hours, compressed workweeks, or job sharing, allow employees to better manage their work-life balance and reduce stress. By empowering employees to have more control over their schedules and work environments, organizations can promote greater work-life balance, autonomy, and well-being.

Additionally, promoting a culture of work-life balance and encouraging employees to take regular breaks and vacations can help prevent burnout and reduce the risk of mental health problems. Encouraging employees to prioritize self-care activities, such as exercise, mindfulness, and hobbies, can also contribute to their overall mental health and resilience. Employers can lead by example by modeling healthy work habits and encouraging employees to prioritize their well-being.

Furthermore, fostering supportive relationships and connections among coworkers can create a sense of belonging and camaraderie in the workplace, which is essential for promoting mental health and well-being. Employers can facilitate team-building activities, social events, or peer support groups to help employees build positive relationships and networks of support. By creating opportunities for social interaction and collaboration, organizations can strengthen employee engagement, morale, and mental health.

Lastly, regularly assessing and evaluating the effectiveness of mental health support initiatives is crucial for ensuring their impact and relevance to employees' needs. Employers can conduct employee surveys, focus groups, or anonymous feedback mechanisms to gather insights and feedback on the effectiveness of existing mental health support programs and identify areas for improvement. By soliciting input from employees and involving them in the decision-making process, organizations can tailor their mental health support initiatives to better meet the needs of their workforce.

In conclusion, promoting mental health support at work is essential for achieving a healthy work environment where employees can thrive both personally and professionally. By offering employee assistance programs, raising awareness, providing flexible work arrangements, promoting work-life balance, fostering supportive relationships, and regularly evaluating initiatives, employers can create a workplace culture that prioritizes mental health and well-being. Ultimately, investing in mental health support not only benefits individual employees but also contributes to organizational success and sustainability.

Encouraging mental health awareness

Encouraging mental health awareness in the workplace is vital for creating a healthy work environment where employees feel supported, valued, and empowered to prioritize their well-being. By promoting mental health awareness, organizations can help reduce stigma, increase understanding, and foster a culture of openness and support around mental health issues.

One effective way to encourage mental health awareness is by providing educational resources and training opportunities for employees. Employers can offer workshops, seminars, or online courses that cover topics such as stress management, resilience-building, coping strategies, and recognizing signs of mental health problems. By equipping employees with knowledge and skills to understand and manage their mental health, organizations empower them to take proactive steps towards maintaining their well-being.

Moreover, incorporating mental health awareness campaigns and initiatives into the workplace can help raise awareness and reduce stigma surrounding mental health issues. Employers can organize events, activities, or awareness campaigns during mental health awareness months, such as Mental Health Awareness Month in May or World Mental Health Day on October 10th. These initiatives can include guest speakers, panel discussions, wellness fairs, mental health screenings, or art and wellness challenges to engage employees and promote dialogue around mental health.

Additionally, leveraging internal communication channels, such as intranet, newsletters, or bulletin boards, can help disseminate information and resources related to mental health awareness. Employers can share articles, podcasts, videos, or personal stories that highlight the importance of mental health, provide tips for self-care, or offer resources for seeking help. By regularly communicating about mental health topics and initiatives, organizations demonstrate their commitment to supporting employee well-being and creating a culture of mental health awareness.

Furthermore, encouraging open and supportive communication about mental health in the workplace can help break down barriers and promote understanding and empathy among colleagues. Employers can create safe spaces, such as support groups or peer networks, where employees feel comfortable sharing their experiences, seeking advice, or offering support to one another. By fostering a culture of openness and support, organizations can help reduce feelings of isolation and encourage individuals to seek help when needed.

Moreover, providing access to mental health resources and support services is essential for promoting mental health awareness and ensuring employees have access to the help they need. Employers can offer employee assistance programs (EAPs), counseling services, mental health hotlines, or online resources where employees can access confidential support and guidance. By making these resources readily available and easily accessible, organizations demonstrate their commitment to supporting employee well-being and promoting mental health awareness.

In conclusion, encouraging mental health awareness in the workplace is crucial for achieving a healthy work environment where employees feel supported, valued, and empowered to prioritize their well-being. By providing educational resources, organizing awareness campaigns, fostering open communication, and offering access to support services, organizations can promote mental health awareness and reduce stigma surrounding mental health issues. Ultimately, investing in mental health awareness benefits both individual employees and the organization as a whole by creating a culture of well-being and resilience.

Providing support systems

Creating and maintaining a healthy work environment involves providing robust support systems that address the diverse needs of employees. These support systems play a crucial role in promoting employee well-being, job satisfaction, and productivity while fostering a culture of support and inclusivity within the organization.

One key aspect of providing support systems in the workplace is offering access to employee assistance programs (EAPs). EAPs are confidential counseling services that provide employees and their families with professional support for various personal and work-related issues, including stress, mental health concerns, substance abuse, financial challenges, and more. By offering EAPs, organizations demonstrate their commitment to supporting employees' holistic well-being and helping them navigate challenging situations effectively.

Moreover, organizations can implement mentorship and coaching programs to provide employees with personalized guidance, career development opportunities, and professional growth. Mentors and coaches can offer valuable insights, advice, and encouragement to help employees navigate career challenges, set goals, develop skills, and achieve their full potential. These programs foster a culture of learning, growth, and support, contributing to employee engagement and retention.

In addition to formal support programs, fostering a culture of peer support and camaraderie is essential for promoting employee well-being and building a sense of community within the workplace. Establishing employee resource groups (ERGs) or affinity groups based on common interests, backgrounds, or experiences allows employees to connect, share experiences, and support one another in a safe and inclusive environment. These groups provide opportunities for networking, mentorship, professional development, and social support, contributing to employee morale and satisfaction.

Furthermore, promoting work-life balance and flexibility is crucial for supporting employee well-being and reducing burnout. Offering flexible work arrangements, such as telecommuting, flexible hours, compressed workweeks, or job sharing, allows employees to better manage their work schedules and personal responsibilities. Additionally, providing paid time off, parental leave, and wellness programs encourages employees to prioritize self-care, recharge, and maintain a healthy work-life balance.

Another essential aspect of providing support systems in the workplace is fostering a culture of recognition and appreciation. Recognizing employees' contributions, achievements, and milestones through formal recognition programs, awards, or incentives reinforces positive behaviors, boosts morale, and strengthens employee engagement. Moreover, fostering a culture of appreciation through regular feedback, praise, and gratitude promotes a positive work environment where employees feel valued, respected, and motivated to perform at their best.

Furthermore, creating a physically and psychologically safe work environment is crucial for supporting employee well-being and promoting a culture of trust and respect. Implementing health and safety protocols, ergonomic workstations, and wellness initiatives helps ensure employees' physical health and comfort. Additionally, fostering open communication, promoting diversity and inclusion, and addressing issues of harassment or discrimination promptly and effectively contribute to a psychologically safe workplace where employees feel respected, supported, and empowered to speak up.

In conclusion, providing robust support systems in the workplace is essential for achieving a healthy work environment where employees feel valued, supported, and empowered to thrive. By offering access to counseling services, mentorship programs, peer support groups, flexible work arrangements, recognition programs, and fostering a culture of trust and respect, organizations can promote employee well-being, job satisfaction, and productivity while cultivating a positive and inclusive workplace culture. Ultimately, investing in support systems benefits both employees and the organization by creating a conducive environment for individual growth, collaboration, and success.

Promoting employee resilience

Promoting employee resilience is a key aspect of achieving a healthy work environment, as it empowers individuals to effectively cope with stress, adversity, and challenges both in their professional and personal lives. Resilience enables employees to bounce back from setbacks, maintain mental and emotional well-being, and adapt to change, ultimately contributing to overall job satisfaction, productivity, and organizational success.

One effective way to promote employee resilience is through the provision of resources and training programs focused on stress management and coping skills. These programs can include workshops, seminars, or online courses that educate employees on techniques such as mindfulness, relaxation exercises, time management, and problem-solving strategies. By equipping employees with practical tools and strategies to manage stress and build resilience, organizations empower them to navigate workplace challenges more effectively and maintain a healthy work-life balance.

Moreover, fostering a culture of support and camaraderie within the workplace is essential for promoting employee resilience. Encouraging teamwork, collaboration, and open communication creates a supportive environment where employees feel comfortable seeking help, sharing concerns, and offering support to one another. Strong social connections and positive relationships with colleagues can serve as a buffer against stress and adversity, enhancing employee resilience and well-being.

Furthermore, providing opportunities for professional development and growth can bolster employee resilience by empowering individuals to build confidence, develop new skills, and adapt to changing roles or responsibilities. Offering training programs, mentorship opportunities, and career advancement pathways allows employees to continuously learn and grow, enhancing their sense of competence and mastery in their roles. Additionally, recognizing and celebrating employees' achievements and milestones reinforces their sense of accomplishment and resilience in the face of challenges.

In addition to individual support, organizational policies and practices play a significant role in promoting employee resilience. Implementing flexible work arrangements, such as remote work options, flexible hours, or compressed workweeks, can help employees better manage their workloads and personal responsibilities, reducing stress and promoting resilience. Moreover, offering comprehensive benefits packages that include mental health resources, counseling services, and wellness programs demonstrates organizational commitment to supporting employee well-being and resilience.

Another important aspect of promoting employee resilience is providing opportunities for autonomy and empowerment in the workplace. Allowing employees to have a voice in decision-making, providing opportunities for skill development and growth, and fostering a culture of trust and accountability empowers individuals to take ownership of their work and build confidence in their abilities. When employees feel empowered and valued, they are better equipped to navigate challenges and setbacks with resilience and determination.

Furthermore, promoting work-life balance and encouraging employees to prioritize self-care activities outside of work can contribute to overall resilience and well-being. Encouraging regular breaks, promoting time off, and supporting activities such as exercise, hobbies, and spending time with loved ones can help employees recharge, reduce stress, and build resilience to workplace challenges.

In conclusion, promoting employee resilience is essential for achieving a healthy work environment where individuals can thrive and succeed. By providing resources and training programs focused on stress management and coping skills, fostering a culture of support and camaraderie, offering opportunities for professional development and growth, implementing flexible work arrangements, and empowering employees in the workplace, organizations can effectively promote resilience and well-being among their workforce. Ultimately, investing in employee resilience benefits both individuals and the organization by enhancing job satisfaction, productivity, and organizational performance.

Building Trust in a Healthy Work Environment

Building trust in a healthy work environment is crucial for fostering positive relationships among employees, enhancing collaboration, and promoting overall organizational success. Trust creates a foundation of mutual respect, transparency, and accountability, allowing individuals to work together effectively and contribute to a supportive and thriving workplace culture.

One essential element of building trust in the workplace is effective communication. Open and transparent communication channels enable employees to share ideas, express concerns, and provide feedback freely. When leaders and managers communicate openly with their teams, they demonstrate honesty, integrity, and respect, fostering an environment of trust and credibility. Regular team meetings, one-on-one discussions, and feedback sessions provide opportunities for employees to voice their opinions, seek clarification, and address any issues or challenges that may arise.

Moreover, demonstrating consistency and reliability in actions and decisions is essential for building trust in the workplace. When leaders and managers consistently follow through on their commitments, uphold organizational values, and treat all employees fairly and equitably, they establish credibility and integrity. Consistency in behavior and decision-making builds confidence among employees, reassuring them that they can rely on their leaders and colleagues to act with integrity and fairness.

Another important aspect of building trust is fostering a culture of collaboration and teamwork. Encouraging collaboration among employees, providing opportunities for cross-functional projects, and recognizing and celebrating team achievements can strengthen relationships and build trust among team members. When employees feel valued and supported by their colleagues, they are more likely to trust and rely on one another, enhancing team cohesion and effectiveness.

Furthermore, empowering employees by delegating authority and involving them in decision-making processes can build trust and confidence in leadership. When employees are given opportunities to contribute their ideas, share their expertise, and participate in decision-making, they feel a sense of ownership and investment in the organization's success. Empowered employees are more likely to trust their leaders and colleagues, knowing that their opinions and contributions are valued and respected.

In addition to fostering trust among employees, organizations must also prioritize building trust with their clients, customers, and other stakeholders. Providing excellent customer service, delivering on promises, and maintaining transparency in business practices are essential for building trust and credibility with external stakeholders. When organizations demonstrate integrity, reliability, and a commitment to ethical business practices, they build strong relationships with their stakeholders, enhancing their reputation and long-term success.

Moreover, establishing clear and fair policies and procedures, and consistently enforcing them, is essential for building trust in the workplace. When employees trust that organizational policies are fair, transparent, and consistently applied, they feel confident in their ability to navigate workplace challenges and conflicts. Clear communication of policies, along with training and support to ensure understanding and compliance, fosters a culture of trust and accountability within the organization.

In conclusion, building trust in a healthy work environment is essential for fostering positive relationships, enhancing collaboration, and promoting organizational success. Effective communication, consistency in actions and decisions, fostering a culture of collaboration and teamwork, empowering employees, prioritizing building trust with external stakeholders, and establishing clear and fair policies and procedures are all essential strategies for building trust in the workplace. By prioritizing trust-building initiatives, organizations can create a positive and supportive work environment where employees feel valued, respected, and empowered to succeed.

Avoiding micromanagement

Micromanagement, a management style characterized by excessive control, close supervision, and an emphasis on minute details, can have detrimental effects on employee morale, productivity, and overall well-being. Avoiding micromanagement is essential for achieving a healthy work environment where employees feel empowered, trusted, and motivated to perform at their best.

One of the key reasons to avoid micromanagement is that it undermines employee autonomy and creativity. When managers excessively monitor and control every aspect of their employees' work, it stifles innovation and discourages initiative. Employees may feel disempowered and demotivated, leading to decreased job satisfaction and morale. Instead of micromanaging, managers should focus on providing clear expectations, setting goals, and empowering employees to make decisions and take ownership of their work.

Furthermore, micromanagement can hinder employee development and growth. When managers constantly dictate tasks and solutions, employees have limited opportunities to learn and develop new skills. Effective leadership involves providing guidance, support, and mentorship to help employees grow and develop professionally. By delegating responsibilities, providing constructive feedback, and offering opportunities for learning and development, managers can empower employees to reach their full potential and contribute meaningfully to the organization.

Moreover, micromanagement can lead to increased stress and burnout among employees. Constant scrutiny and pressure to meet unrealistic expectations can take a toll on employee mental health and well-being. High levels of stress can result in decreased job satisfaction, increased absenteeism, and higher turnover rates. To avoid micromanagement, managers should focus on building trusting relationships with their employees, providing support, and recognizing and appreciating their efforts and contributions.

Additionally, micromanagement can create a culture of distrust and resentment in the workplace. When employees feel that their every move is being scrutinized and questioned, it erodes trust and damages the manager-employee relationship. Trust is essential for fostering collaboration, communication, and teamwork in the workplace. Managers should focus on building trust by demonstrating confidence in their employees' abilities, respecting their expertise, and providing opportunities for autonomy and growth.

Furthermore, micromanagement can hinder organizational agility and flexibility. In today's fast-paced and dynamic business environment, organizations need to be able to adapt quickly to changing market conditions and customer needs. Micromanagement can slow down decision-making processes and impede innovation, making it difficult for organizations to respond effectively to challenges and opportunities. By empowering employees to make decisions and take calculated risks, organizations can foster a culture of agility and adaptability that enables them to thrive in a competitive landscape.

In conclusion, avoiding micromanagement is essential for achieving a healthy work environment where employees feel empowered, motivated, and supported to perform at their best. By focusing on building trust, empowering employees, providing opportunities for growth and development, and fostering a culture of autonomy and collaboration, organizations can create an environment where employees thrive and contribute meaningfully to organizational success. Effective leadership involves striking a balance between providing guidance and support while allowing employees the freedom to innovate, take ownership, and grow professionally.

Encouraging mutual respect

Encouraging mutual respect in the workplace is paramount for fostering a healthy work environment where employees feel valued, appreciated, and empowered to collaborate effectively towards common goals. Mutual respect entails recognizing the dignity, worth, and contributions of each individual, regardless of their position or background, and treating others with kindness, empathy, and professionalism.

One of the key benefits of encouraging mutual respect in the workplace is the creation of a positive organizational culture. When employees feel respected and valued by their peers and supervisors, they are more likely to feel motivated, engaged, and committed to their work. A culture of respect promotes trust, open communication, and teamwork, which are essential for achieving organizational objectives and driving success.

Moreover, mutual respect enhances employee morale and job satisfaction. When employees feel respected and appreciated for their contributions, they experience greater job satisfaction and are more likely to be loyal to the organization. Respectful interactions and positive relationships among colleagues contribute to a supportive and inclusive work environment where employees feel happy, fulfilled, and motivated to excel in their roles.

Furthermore, encouraging mutual respect fosters diversity and inclusion in the workplace. Respect for diversity involves recognizing and embracing the unique perspectives, backgrounds, and experiences of all employees. By promoting an inclusive culture where differences are celebrated and valued, organizations can leverage the diverse talents and perspectives of their workforce to drive innovation, creativity, and competitiveness.

In addition, mutual respect contributes to effective conflict resolution and problem-solving. When employees approach disagreements and challenges with respect and empathy, they are more likely to engage in constructive dialogue, seek common ground, and find mutually acceptable solutions. Respectful communication and collaboration enable teams to overcome obstacles and achieve shared goals in a productive and harmonious manner.

Furthermore, mutual respect enhances leadership effectiveness. Leaders who demonstrate respect for their employees inspire trust, loyalty, and commitment. Respectful leaders listen to their employees' perspectives, provide support and guidance, and empower them to reach their full potential. By leading with integrity, humility, and compassion, leaders can cultivate a culture of respect that fosters high performance, innovation, and organizational success.

Additionally, encouraging mutual respect helps to mitigate workplace conflicts and reduce instances of harassment, discrimination, and bullying. When employees treat each other with respect and professionalism, they are less likely to engage in behaviors that harm others or create a hostile work environment. Organizations can establish clear policies and procedures to address disrespectful behavior and promote a culture of respect and civility in the workplace.

In conclusion, encouraging mutual respect is essential for achieving a healthy work environment where employees feel valued, supported, and empowered to thrive. By promoting respect for diversity, fostering positive relationships, and modeling respectful behavior at all levels of the organization, organizations can create a culture of respect that enhances employee morale, engagement, and productivity. Mutual respect is not only a fundamental human value but also a key driver of organizational success and sustainability.

Ensuring transparency

Transparency in the workplace is a cornerstone of achieving a healthy work environment. It involves open, honest, and clear communication between employees and management, as well as the sharing of information regarding organizational decisions, policies, and processes. By prioritizing transparency, organizations can foster trust, accountability, and collaboration among employees, leading to increased morale, engagement, and productivity.

One of the primary benefits of ensuring transparency in the workplace is the promotion of trust and credibility. When employees are kept informed about the company's goals, strategies, and performance, they feel more confident in the organization's leadership and direction. Transparent communication builds trust between employees and management, as it demonstrates a commitment to honesty, integrity, and fairness in decision-making processes.

Moreover, transparency enhances employee engagement and empowerment. When employees have access to relevant information about their roles, responsibilities, and performance expectations, they are better equipped to make informed decisions and take ownership of their work. Transparent communication fosters a sense of inclusion and involvement, as employees feel valued and respected when their opinions and feedback are considered in decision-making processes.

Furthermore, ensuring transparency in the workplace promotes accountability and ethical behavior. By openly sharing information about company policies, procedures, and performance metrics, organizations hold employees accountable for their actions and encourage adherence to ethical standards and values. Transparency also helps to identify and address issues or concerns promptly, preventing potential misconduct or unethical behavior.

Additionally, transparency contributes to effective problem-solving and decision-making processes. When employees have access to relevant information and are involved in discussions regarding organizational challenges or opportunities, they can contribute valuable insights and perspectives to the decision-making process. Transparent communication encourages collaboration and innovation, as employees feel empowered to share ideas, ask questions, and challenge assumptions in a supportive and respectful environment.

Furthermore, transparency in the workplace promotes a culture of continuous learning and improvement. By openly sharing successes, failures, and lessons learned, organizations create opportunities for growth and development at all levels. Transparent communication encourages employees to embrace feedback, seek new knowledge and skills, and adapt to changing circumstances, fostering a culture of resilience and agility in the face of challenges.

Moreover, ensuring transparency in the workplace helps to build a positive employer brand and attract top talent. Organizations that prioritize transparency demonstrate a commitment to integrity, fairness, and accountability, which can enhance their reputation as an employer of choice. Transparent communication about company values, culture, and opportunities for growth can help organizations attract and retain highly skilled and motivated employees who align with their mission and vision.

In conclusion, ensuring transparency in the workplace is essential for achieving a healthy work environment where employees feel valued, empowered, and motivated to succeed. By prioritizing open, honest, and clear communication, organizations can build trust, accountability, and collaboration among employees, leading to increased engagement, productivity, and satisfaction. Transparent communication fosters a culture of inclusion, learning, and continuous improvement, driving organizational success and sustainability in the long term.

Sustainability in the Workplace

Sustainability in the workplace is a crucial aspect of achieving a healthy work environment. It involves adopting practices and policies that minimize negative environmental impacts, promote social responsibility, and contribute to long-term economic viability. By prioritizing sustainability initiatives, organizations can enhance employee well-being, reduce operational costs, and demonstrate a commitment to environmental stewardship.

One of the primary benefits of incorporating sustainability practices into the workplace is the promotion of employee well-being. Sustainable initiatives such as green building design, access to natural light, and indoor air quality improvements can create a healthier and more comfortable work environment for employees. Studies have shown that exposure to natural elements and environmentally friendly design features can reduce stress, increase productivity, and enhance overall job satisfaction among employees.

Moreover, sustainability initiatives in the workplace can help reduce operational costs and increase efficiency. Implementing energy-efficient lighting, heating, and cooling systems, as well as water-saving measures, can lead to significant cost savings over time. Additionally, adopting sustainable procurement practices and waste reduction strategies can minimize resource consumption and waste generation, further reducing operating expenses and enhancing financial performance.

Furthermore, incorporating sustainability into the workplace promotes social responsibility and community engagement. By supporting local suppliers, investing in community development projects, and promoting diversity and inclusion, organizations can positively impact the communities in which they operate. Sustainable business practices also contribute to the overall well-being of society by reducing pollution, conserving natural resources, and mitigating climate change.

Additionally, sustainability initiatives in the workplace can enhance brand reputation and attract environmentally conscious customers and employees. Organizations that prioritize sustainability demonstrate a commitment to environmental stewardship and social responsibility, which can differentiate them from competitors and build trust and loyalty among stakeholders. Sustainability initiatives can also help organizations attract and retain top talent by appealing to employees who are passionate about making a positive impact on the environment and society.

Furthermore, sustainability in the workplace contributes to long-term economic viability and resilience. By reducing reliance on finite resources, minimizing environmental risks, and adapting to changing regulatory requirements and consumer preferences, organizations can position themselves for sustainable growth and success in the future. Sustainable business practices also help mitigate operational risks associated with environmental and social issues, such as resource scarcity, regulatory non-compliance, and reputational damage.

Moreover, incorporating sustainability into the workplace fosters a culture of innovation and continuous improvement. By encouraging employees to identify and implement sustainable solutions, organizations can harness the creativity and expertise of their workforce to address complex environmental and social challenges. Sustainable initiatives also provide opportunities for collaboration and knowledge sharing among employees, leading to new ideas, insights, and best practices that drive organizational success.

In conclusion, sustainability in the workplace is essential for achieving a healthy work environment that promotes employee well-being, reduces operational costs, and demonstrates social responsibility. By incorporating sustainable practices and policies, organizations can create a positive impact on the environment, society, and economy while positioning themselves for long-term success and resilience.

Going green for better productivity

Going green in the workplace can significantly contribute to achieving a healthy work environment and enhancing productivity. By adopting sustainable practices and initiatives, organizations can reduce their environmental footprint, improve employee well-being, and boost overall productivity levels.

One way that going green can enhance productivity is by creating a healthier work environment. Green initiatives such as improving indoor air quality, incorporating natural light, and using environmentally friendly materials can contribute to better employee health and well-being. Research has shown that exposure to natural elements and green spaces can reduce stress, increase concentration, and enhance overall job satisfaction, ultimately leading to higher levels of productivity among employees.

Moreover, implementing energy-efficient measures can lead to cost savings and increased efficiency, further contributing to productivity. By optimizing energy use, organizations can reduce utility bills and allocate resources more efficiently. Energy-efficient lighting, heating, and cooling systems not only reduce operational costs but also create a more comfortable and conducive work environment, allowing employees to focus better on their tasks and perform more effectively.

Additionally, going green can foster a culture of innovation and creativity within the workplace. Sustainable initiatives encourage employees to think critically about resource consumption, waste reduction, and environmental impact, leading to the development of innovative solutions and practices. By promoting a culture of sustainability, organizations can inspire employees to identify opportunities for improvement, implement new ideas, and contribute to continuous innovation and growth.

Furthermore, going green can enhance employee morale and engagement, leading to higher levels of productivity. Employees are more likely to feel motivated and fulfilled when they work for an organization that prioritizes environmental sustainability and social responsibility. Green initiatives such as eco-friendly policies, recycling programs, and volunteer opportunities can foster a sense of purpose and pride among employees, leading to increased job satisfaction and commitment to organizational goals.

Moreover, adopting sustainable practices can improve the company's reputation and attractiveness to customers and stakeholders. In today's environmentally conscious marketplace, consumers prefer to support businesses that prioritize sustainability and environmental responsibility. By going green, organizations can differentiate themselves from competitors, build trust and loyalty among customers, and attract environmentally conscious consumers who are willing to pay a premium for sustainable products and services.

Additionally, going green can help organizations comply with regulatory requirements and stay ahead of emerging environmental trends and regulations. By proactively addressing environmental issues and implementing sustainable practices, organizations can minimize the risk of non-compliance, avoid costly fines and penalties, and maintain a positive reputation in the marketplace.

In conclusion, going green in the workplace is essential for achieving a healthy work environment and enhancing productivity. By adopting sustainable practices and initiatives, organizations can create a healthier, more efficient, and more innovative workplace that fosters employee well-being, engagement, and productivity. Moreover, going green can improve the company's reputation, attract environmentally conscious customers, and position the organization for long-term success and sustainability.

Encouraging employee involvement

Encouraging employee involvement is crucial for achieving a healthy work environment and fostering a culture of collaboration, innovation, and engagement within the organization. When employees feel valued, empowered, and involved in decision-making processes, they are more likely to be motivated, satisfied, and productive in their roles.

One way to encourage employee involvement is by creating opportunities for open communication and feedback. Organizations can establish channels such as suggestion boxes, employee forums, and regular meetings to encourage employees to share their ideas, concerns, and feedback on various aspects of their work environment. By actively listening to employees' perspectives and incorporating their input into decision-making processes, organizations can demonstrate their commitment to valuing employee opinions and fostering a culture of inclusivity and collaboration.

Moreover, involving employees in goal-setting and planning processes can increase their sense of ownership and commitment to organizational objectives. By allowing employees to participate in setting performance goals, identifying priorities, and developing action plans, organizations can ensure alignment between individual and organizational objectives and empower employees to take ownership of their work and contribute to achieving shared goals.

Furthermore, promoting employee involvement in problem-solving and decision-making processes can lead to more effective and sustainable solutions. Organizations can encourage employees to participate in cross-functional teams, task forces, or committees to address specific challenges, develop innovative solutions, and drive continuous improvement initiatives. By leveraging the diverse perspectives, skills, and experiences of employees, organizations can identify root causes, explore alternative approaches, and implement solutions that address complex problems more effectively.

Additionally, providing opportunities for skill development and training can empower employees to take on new responsibilities and contribute to organizational success. By investing in employee development programs, workshops, and training sessions, organizations can equip employees with the knowledge, skills, and tools they need to excel in their roles and make meaningful contributions to the organization. Empowering employees to develop and grow professionally not only enhances their job satisfaction and engagement but also strengthens the organization's talent pipeline and capacity for innovation and growth.

Moreover, recognizing and rewarding employee contributions can reinforce a culture of involvement and engagement within the organization. Organizations can implement recognition programs, rewards systems, or peer-to-peer recognition initiatives to celebrate employee achievements, contributions, and milestones. By acknowledging and appreciating employees' efforts and accomplishments, organizations can reinforce positive behaviors, boost morale, and cultivate a culture of appreciation, respect, and teamwork.

Furthermore, promoting a sense of belonging and inclusion can encourage employee involvement and engagement. Organizations can create opportunities for employees to connect, collaborate, and build relationships with colleagues through team-building activities, social events, and networking opportunities. By fostering a sense of community and belonging, organizations can create a supportive and inclusive work environment where employees feel valued, respected, and motivated to contribute their best work.

In conclusion, encouraging employee involvement is essential for achieving a healthy work environment and fostering a culture of collaboration, innovation, and engagement within the organization. By creating opportunities for open communication, involving employees in goal-setting and decision-making processes, providing opportunities for skill development and training, recognizing and rewarding employee contributions, and promoting a sense of belonging and inclusion, organizations can empower employees to thrive and contribute to organizational success.

Have Questions / Comments?

This book was designed to cover as much as possible but I know I have probably missed something, or some new amazing discovery that has just come out.

If you notice something missing or have a question that I failed to answer, please get in touch and let me know. If I can, I will email you an answer and also update the book so others can also benefit from it.

Thanks For Being Awesome :)

Submit Your Questions / Comments At:

https://xspurts.com/posts/questions

Get Another Book Free

We love writing and have produced a huge number of books.

For being one of our amazing readers, we would love to offer you another book we have created, 100% free.

To claim this limited time special offer, simply go to the site below and enter your name and email address.

You will then receive one of my great books, direct to your email account, 100% free!

https://xspurts.com/posts/free-book-offer